Christmas Toddler Coloring Book

First edition: 2017
Photo credit: Shutterstock

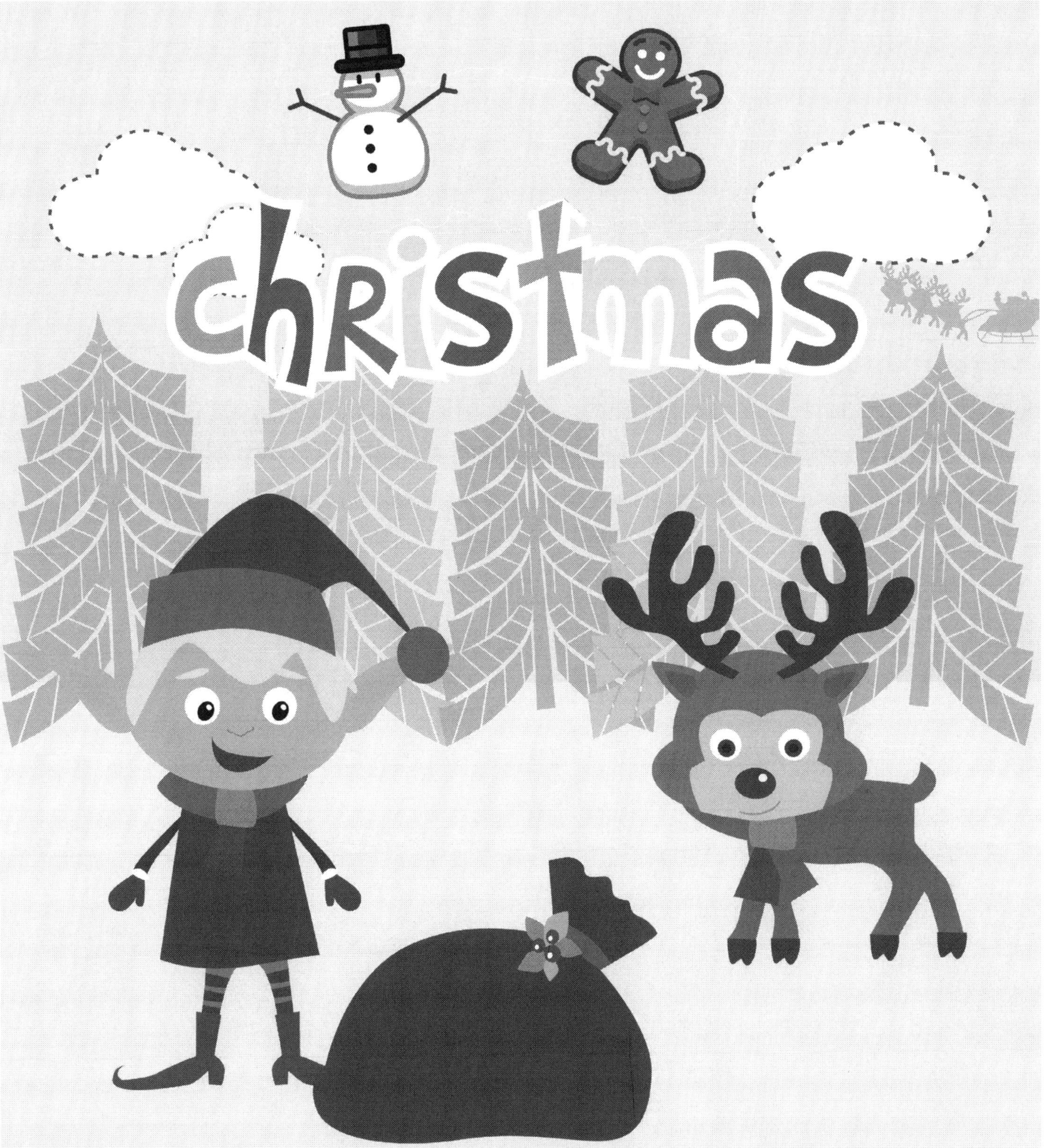

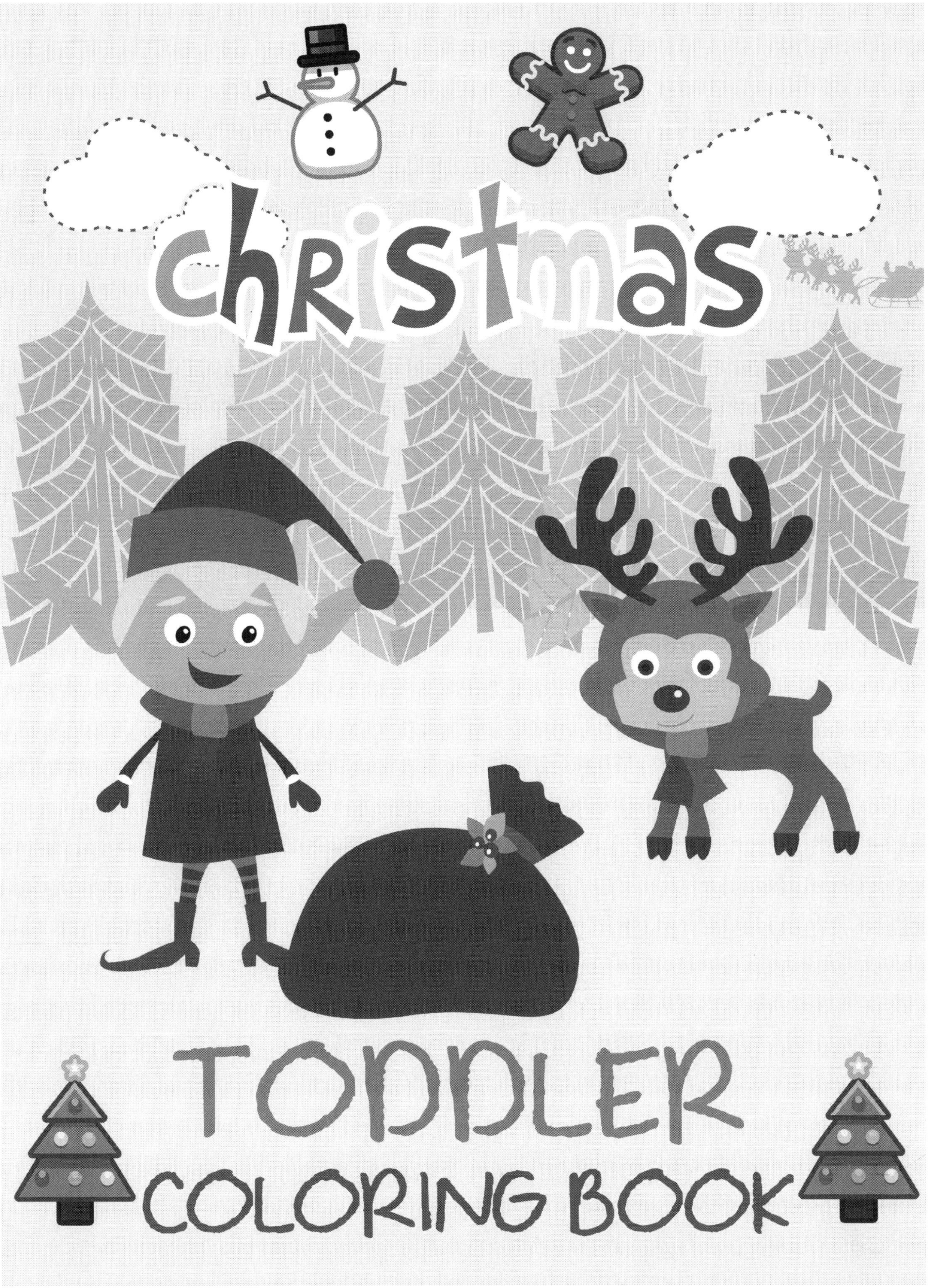

TODDLER
COLORING BOOK

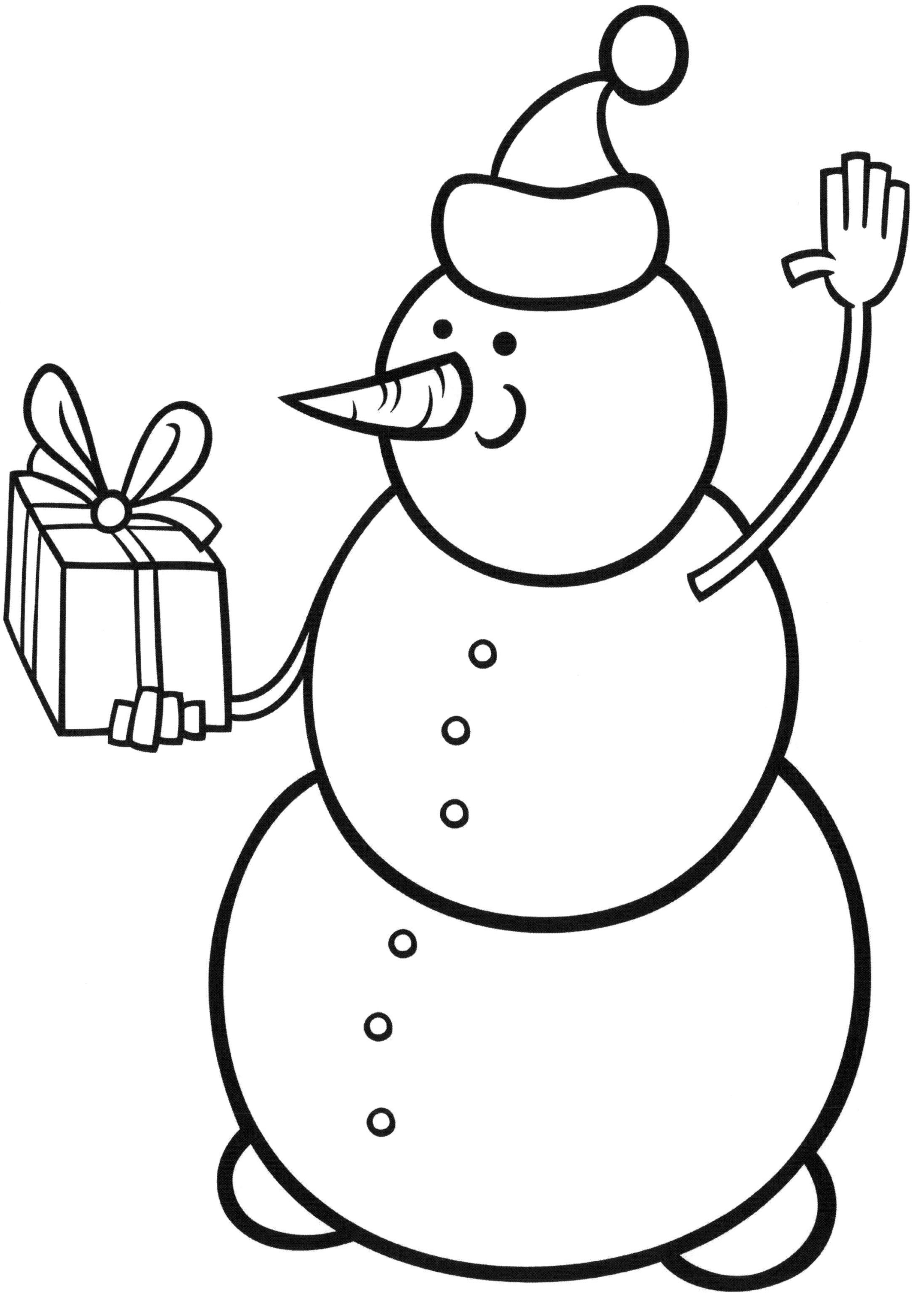

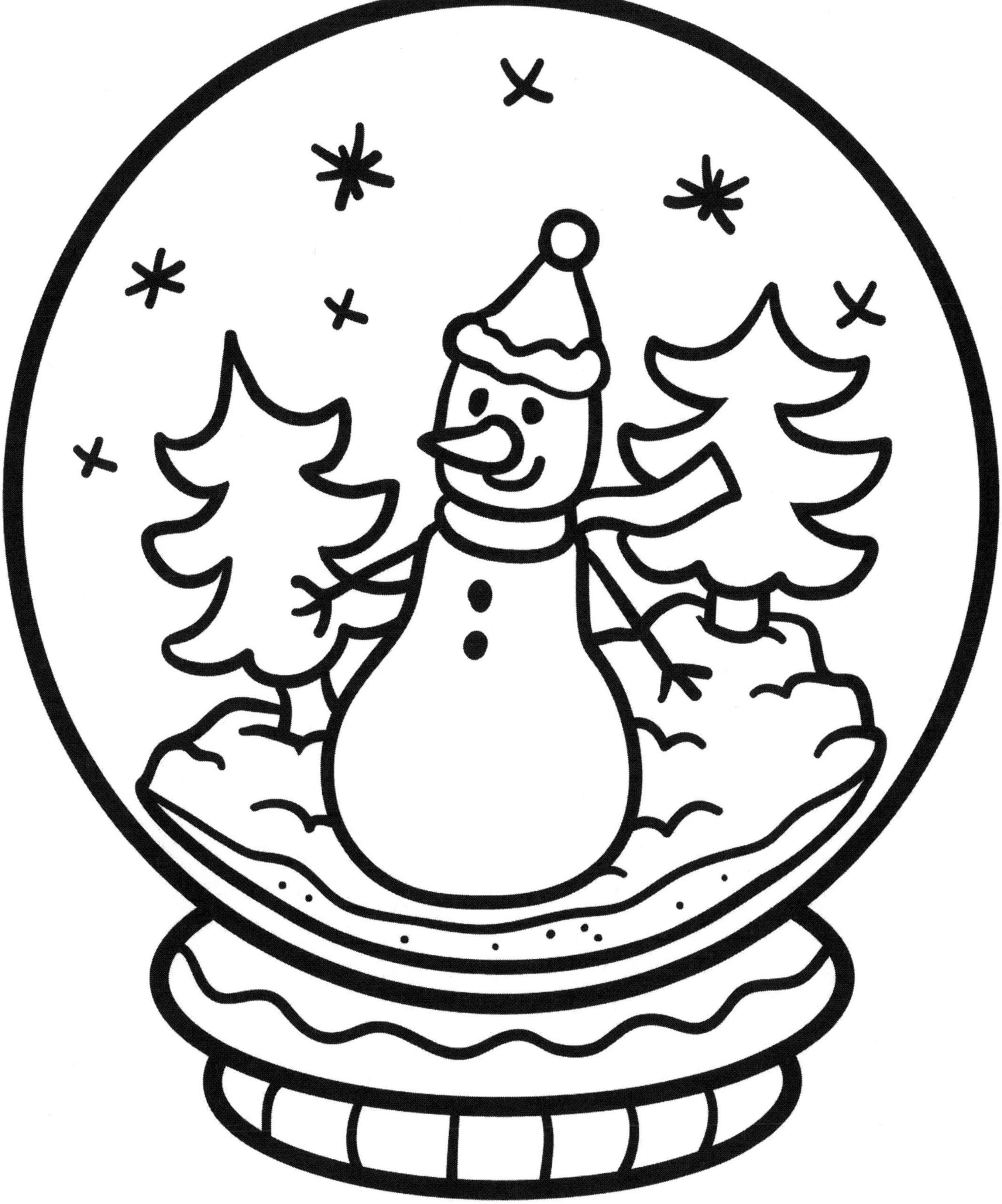

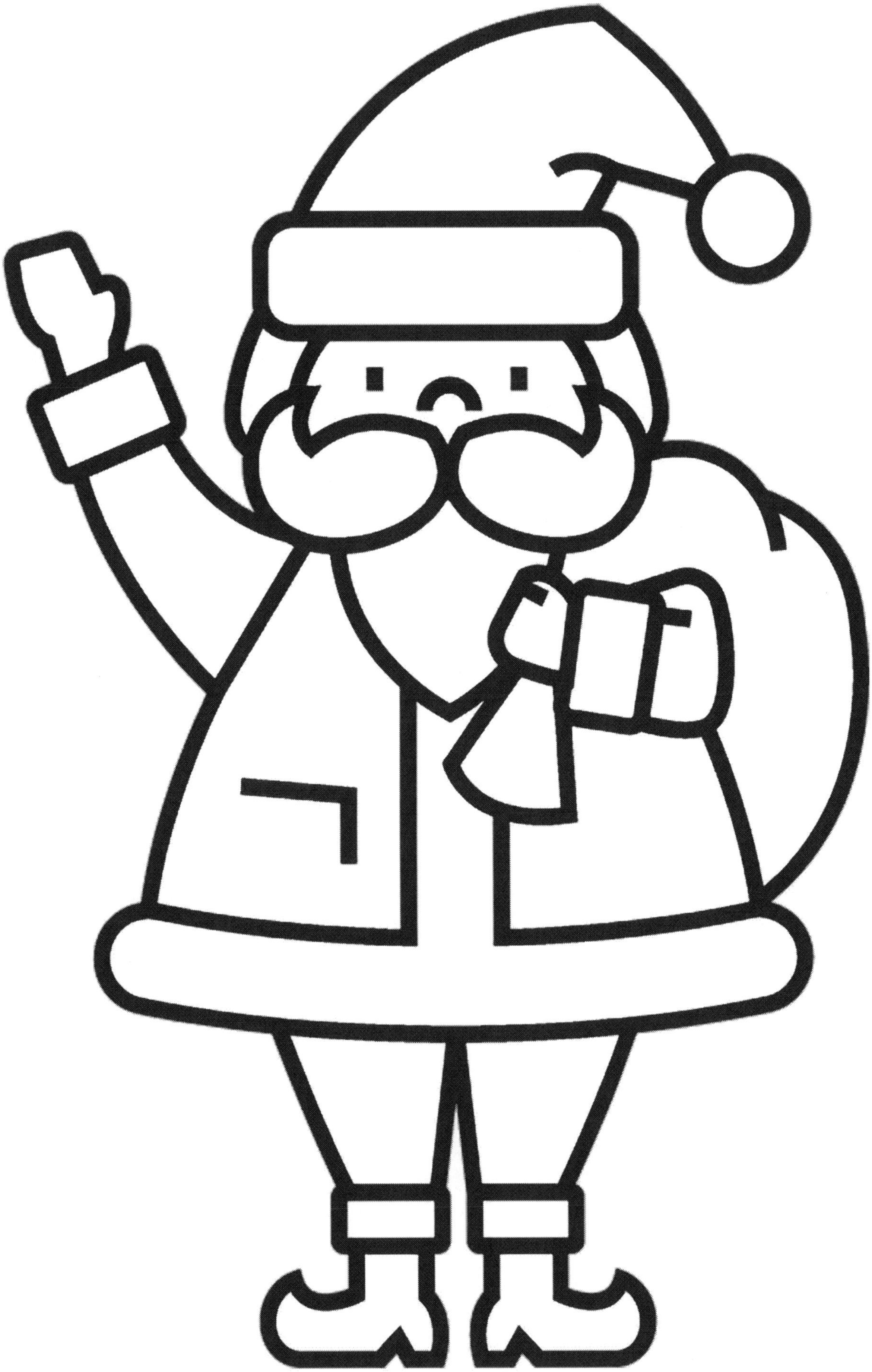

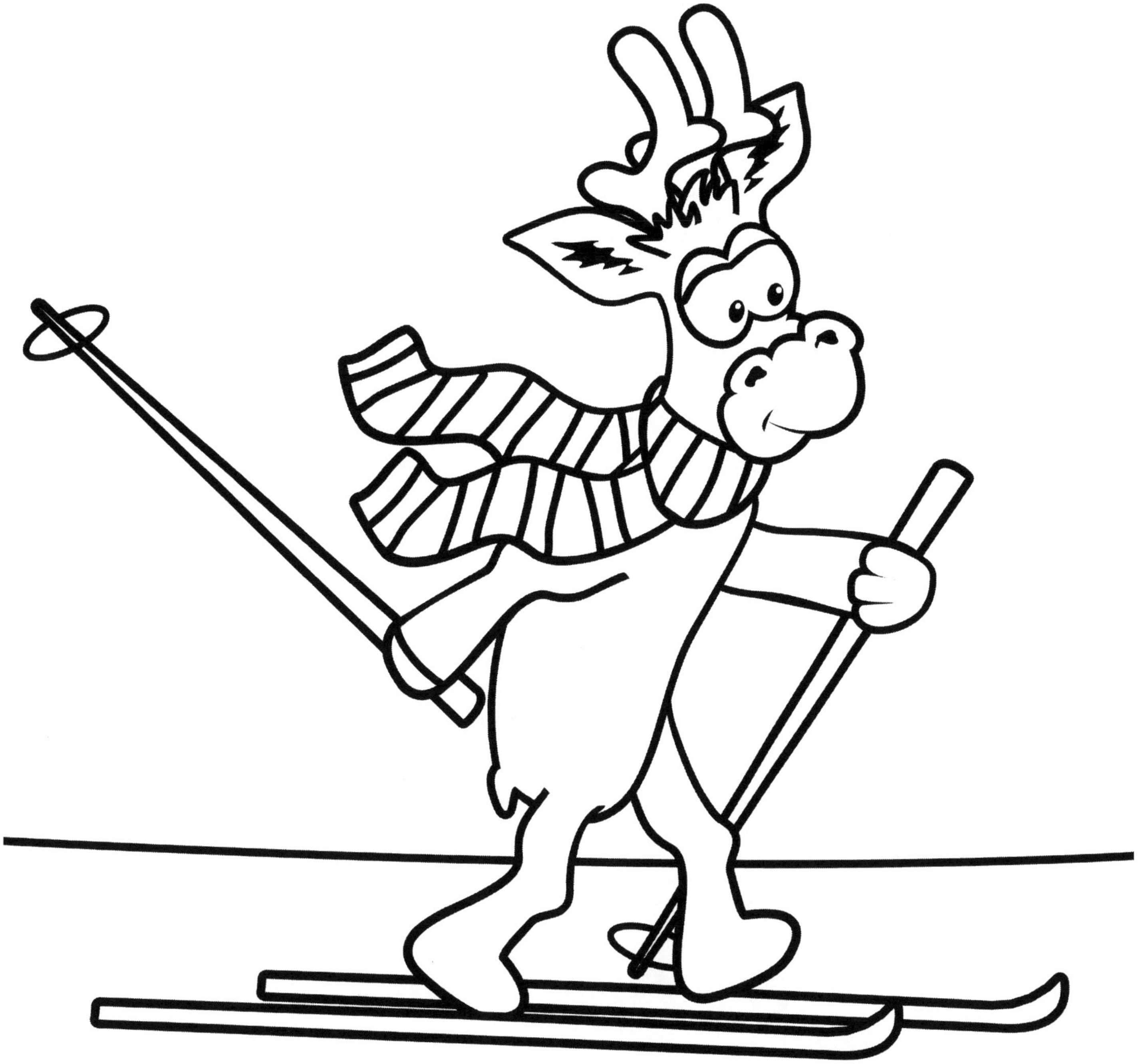

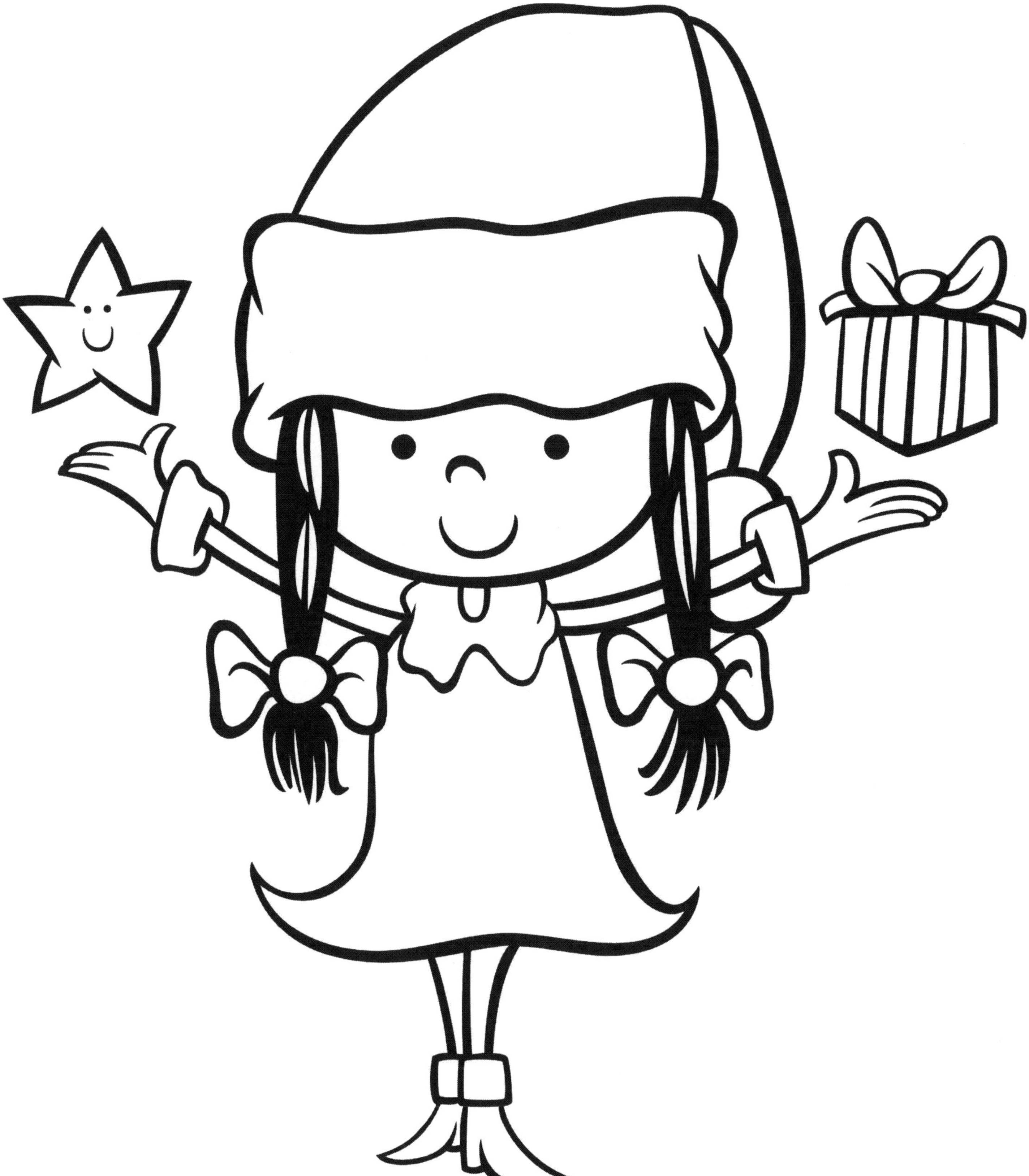

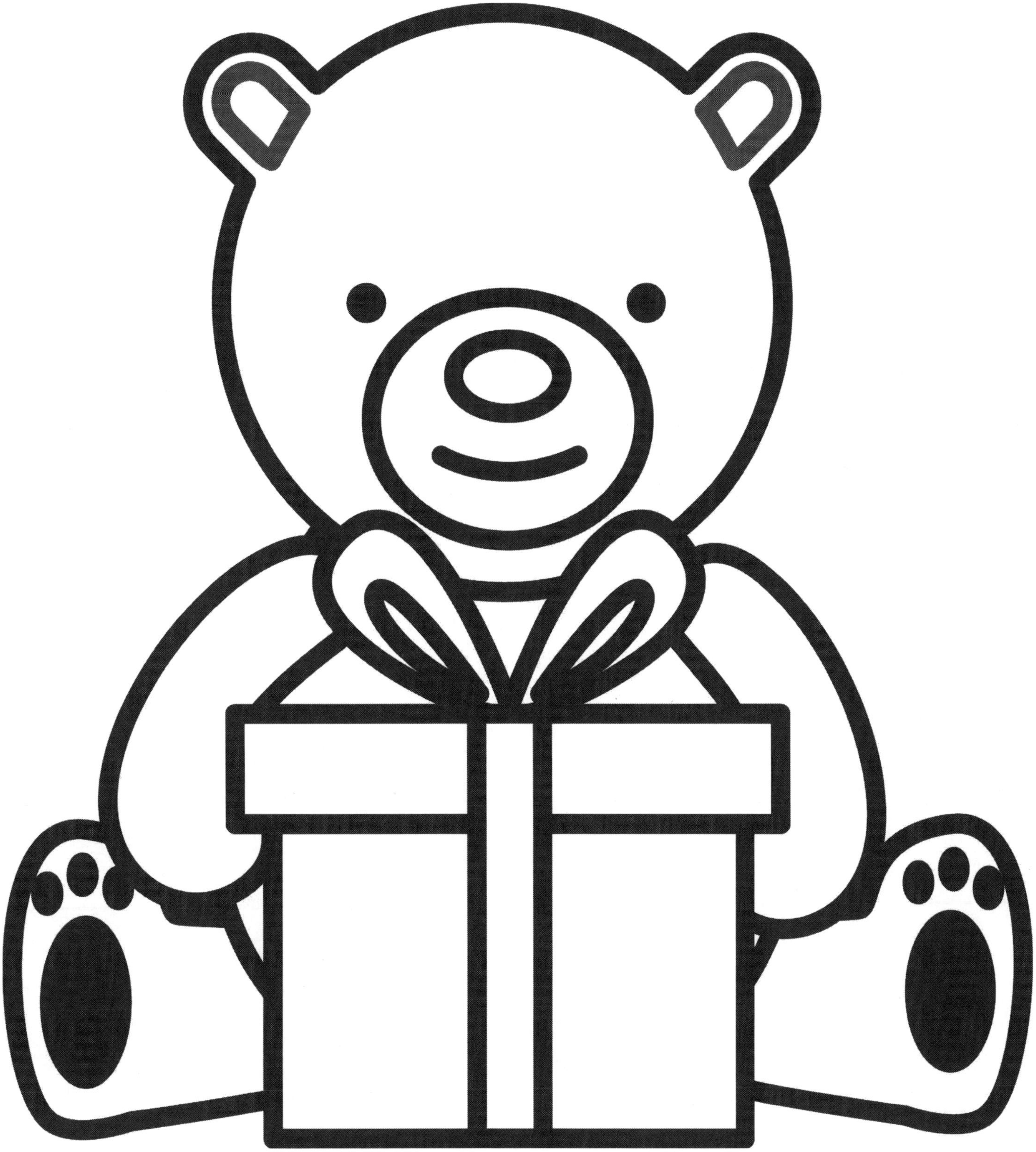

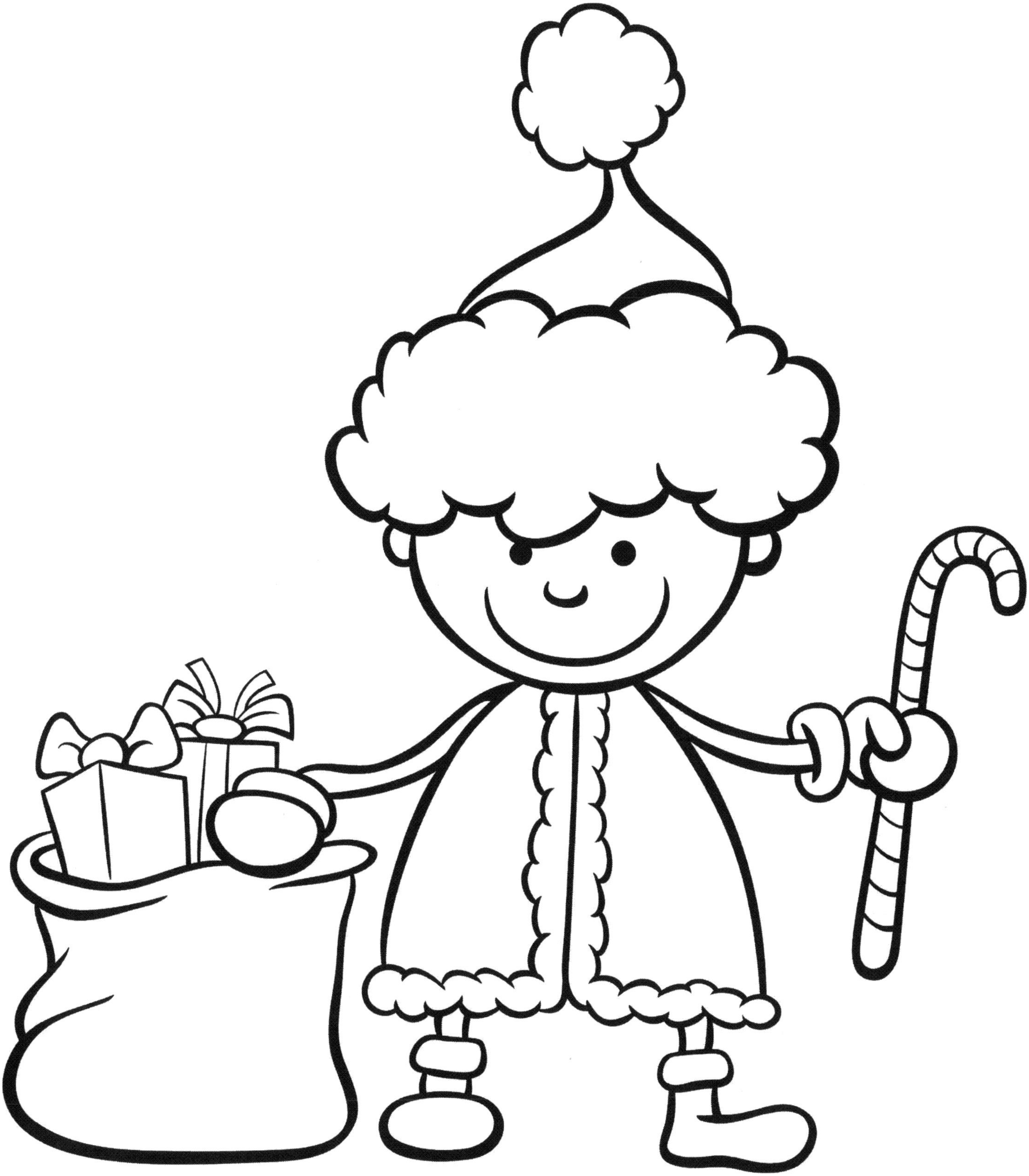

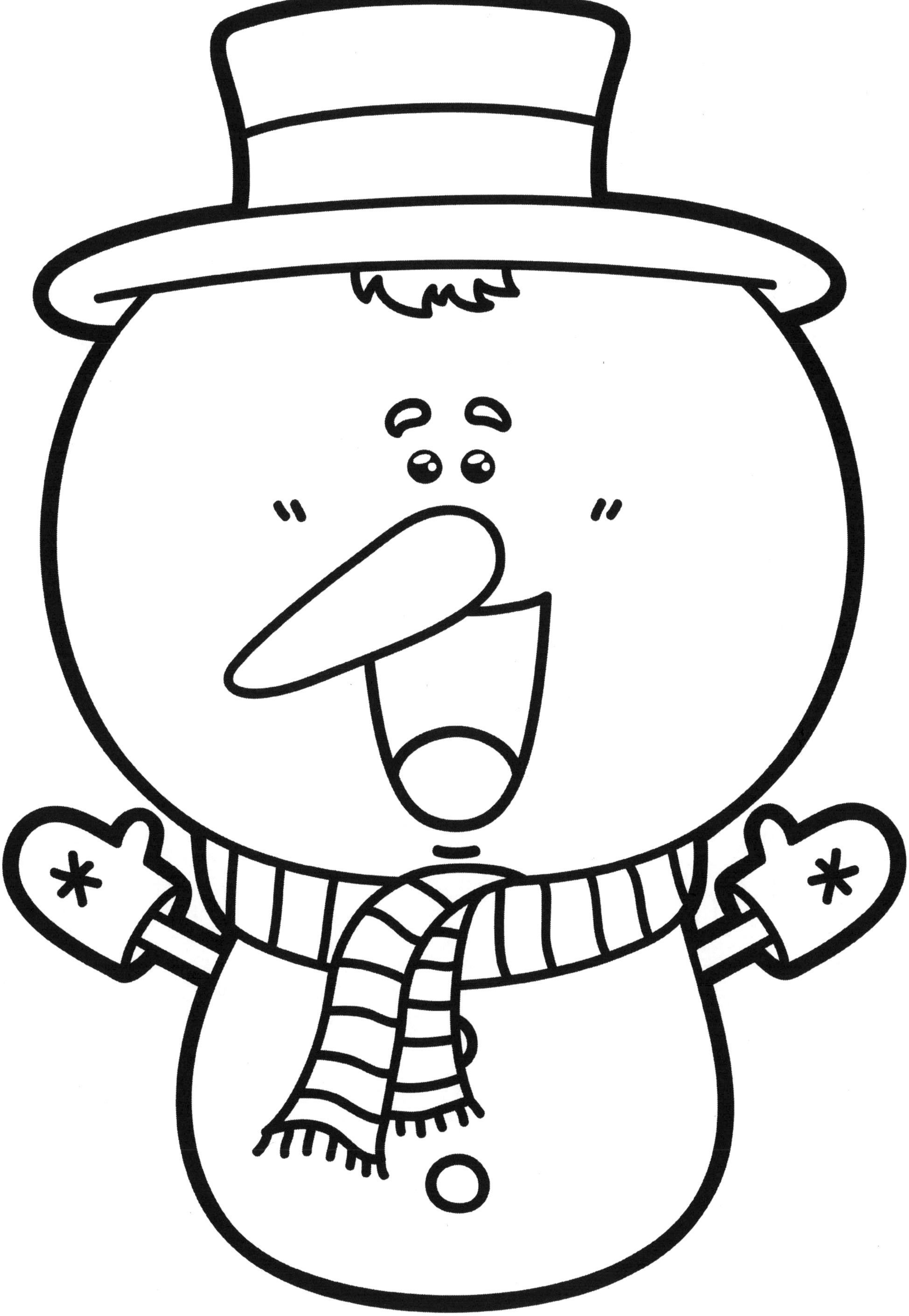

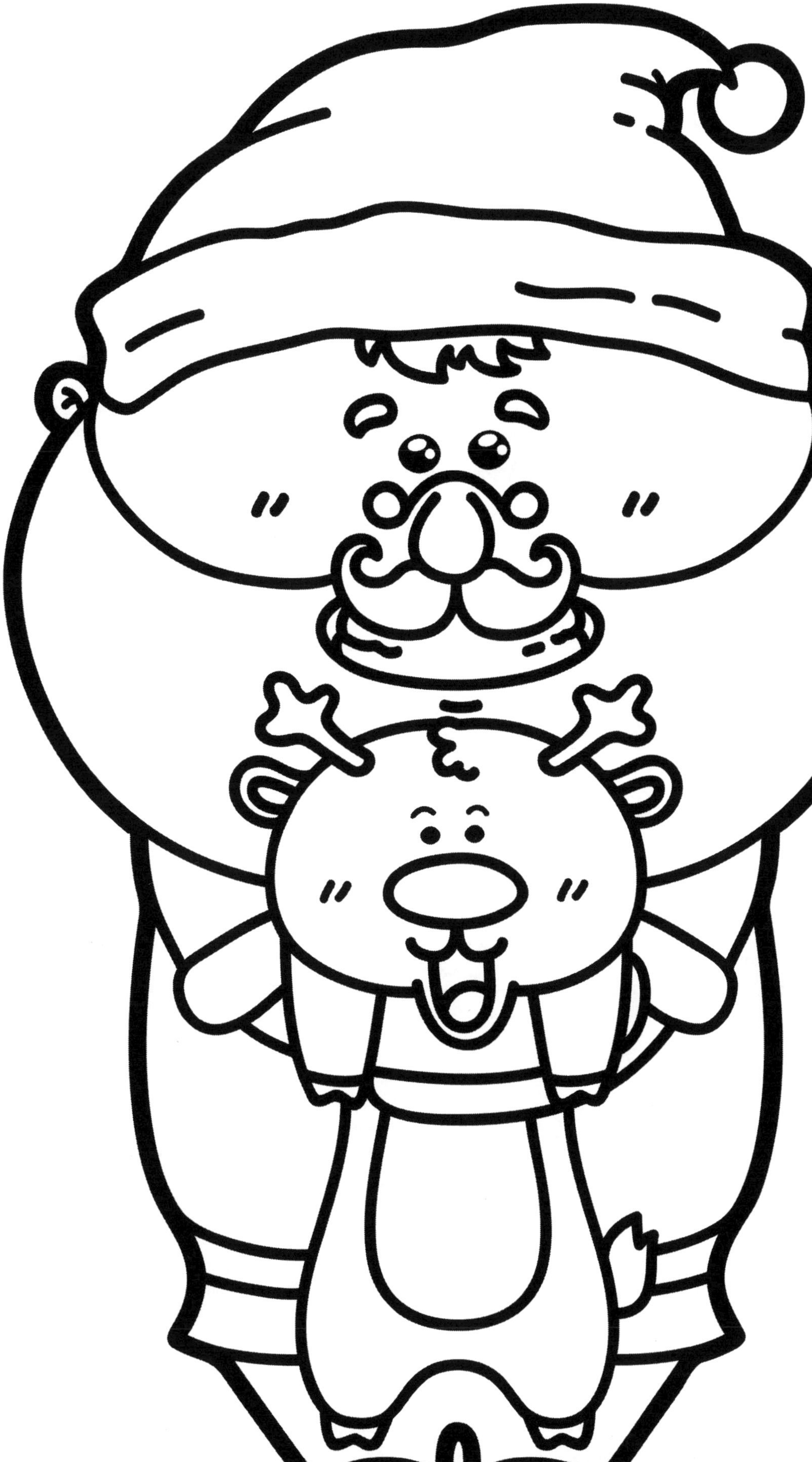

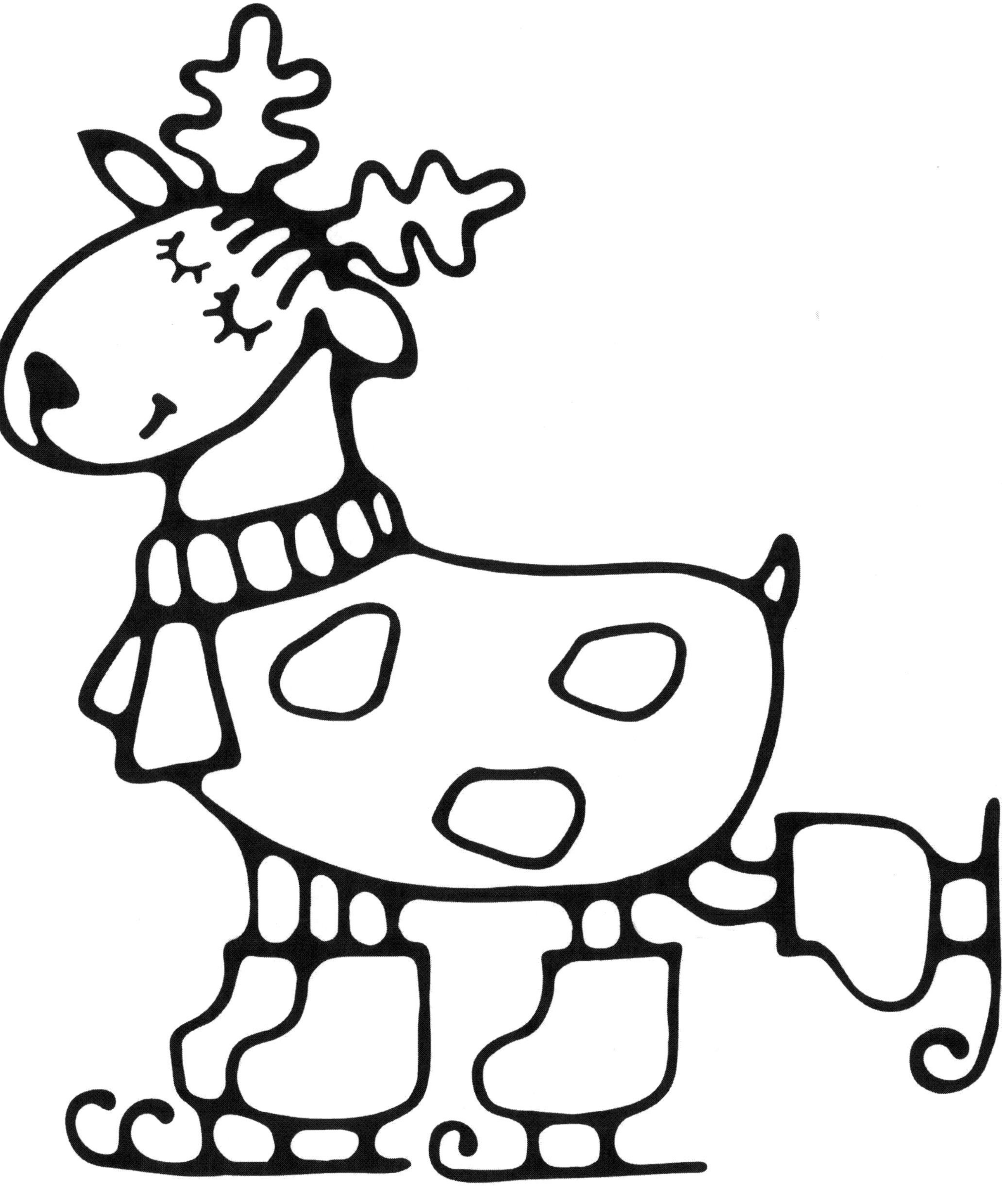

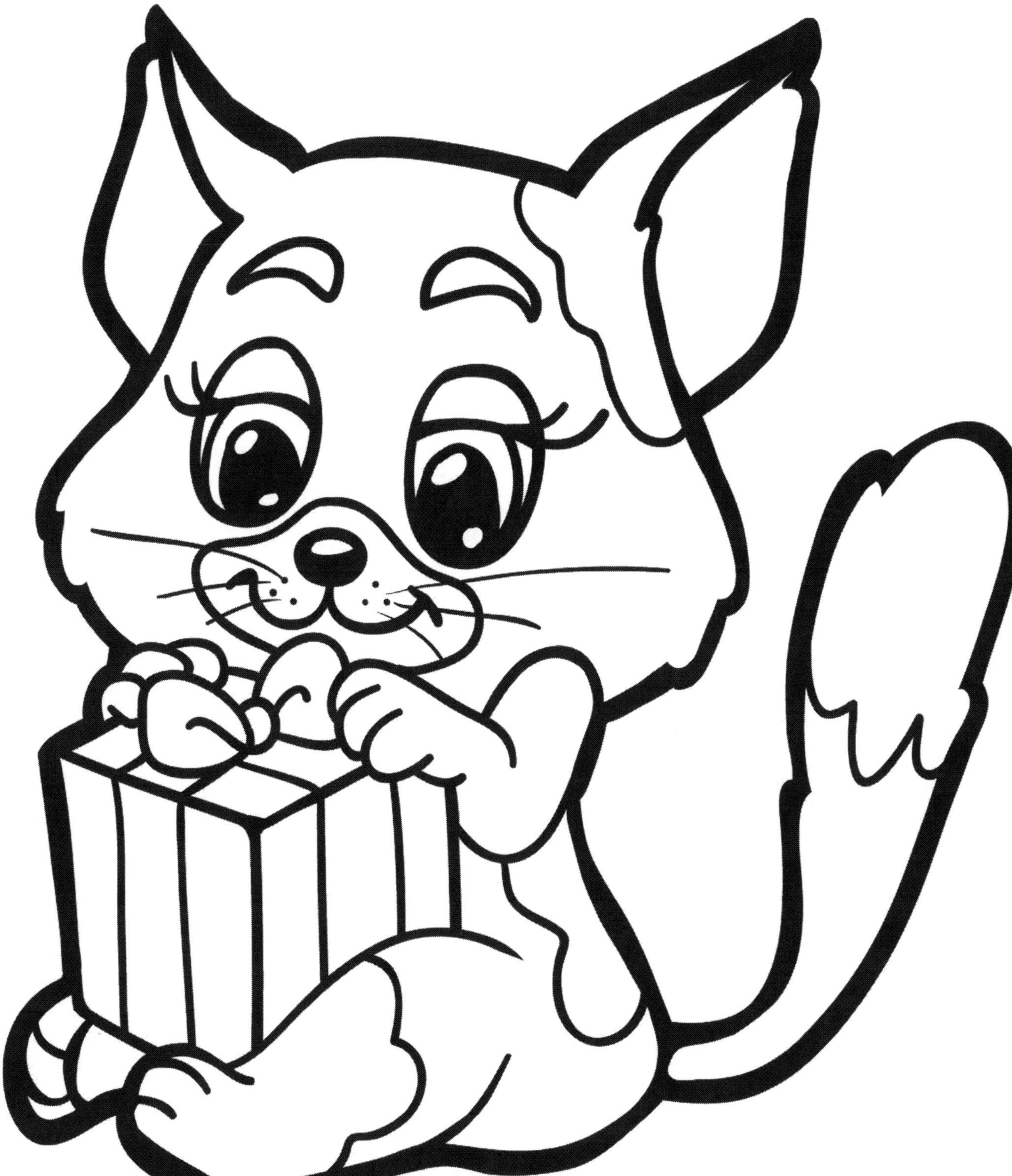

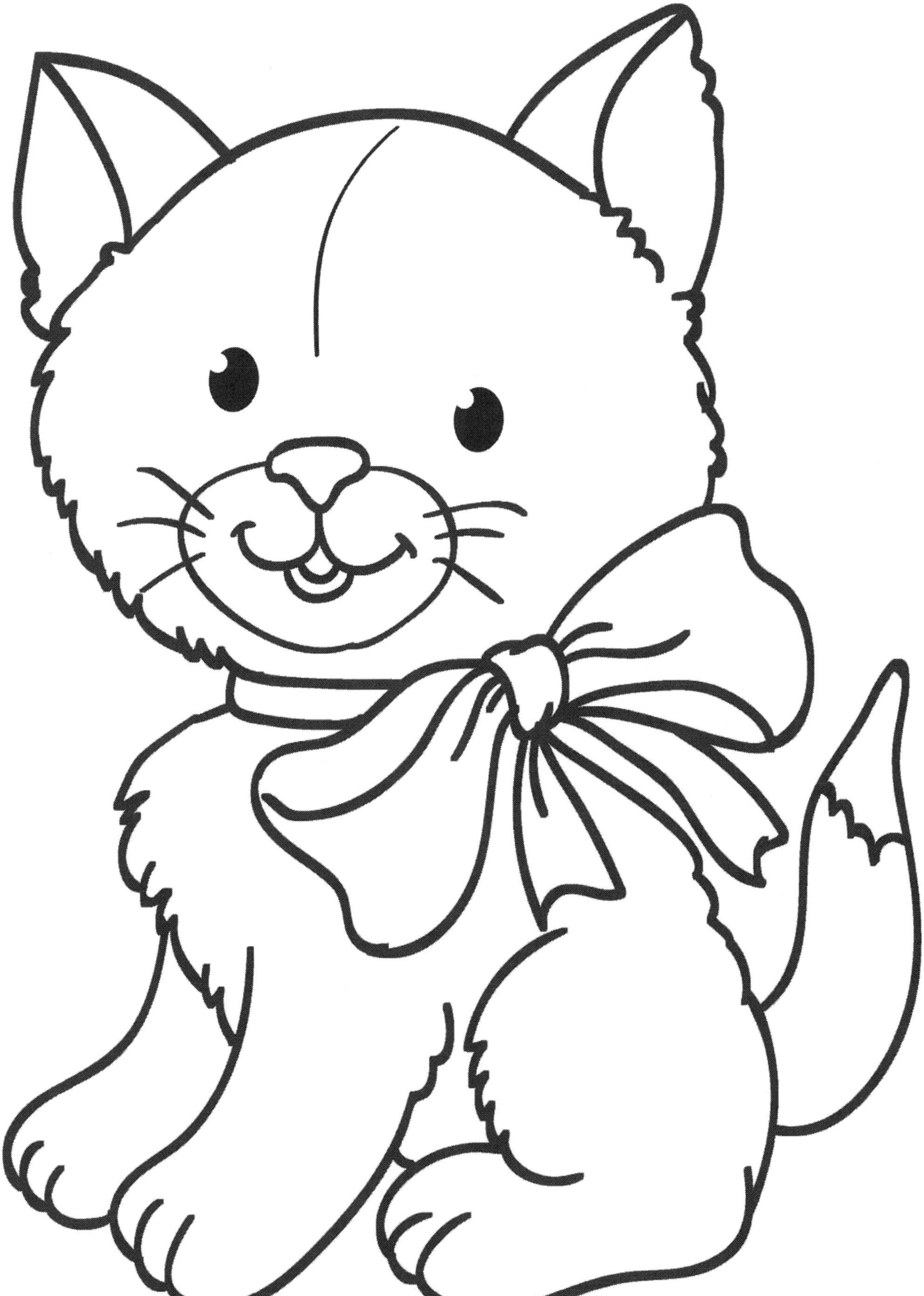

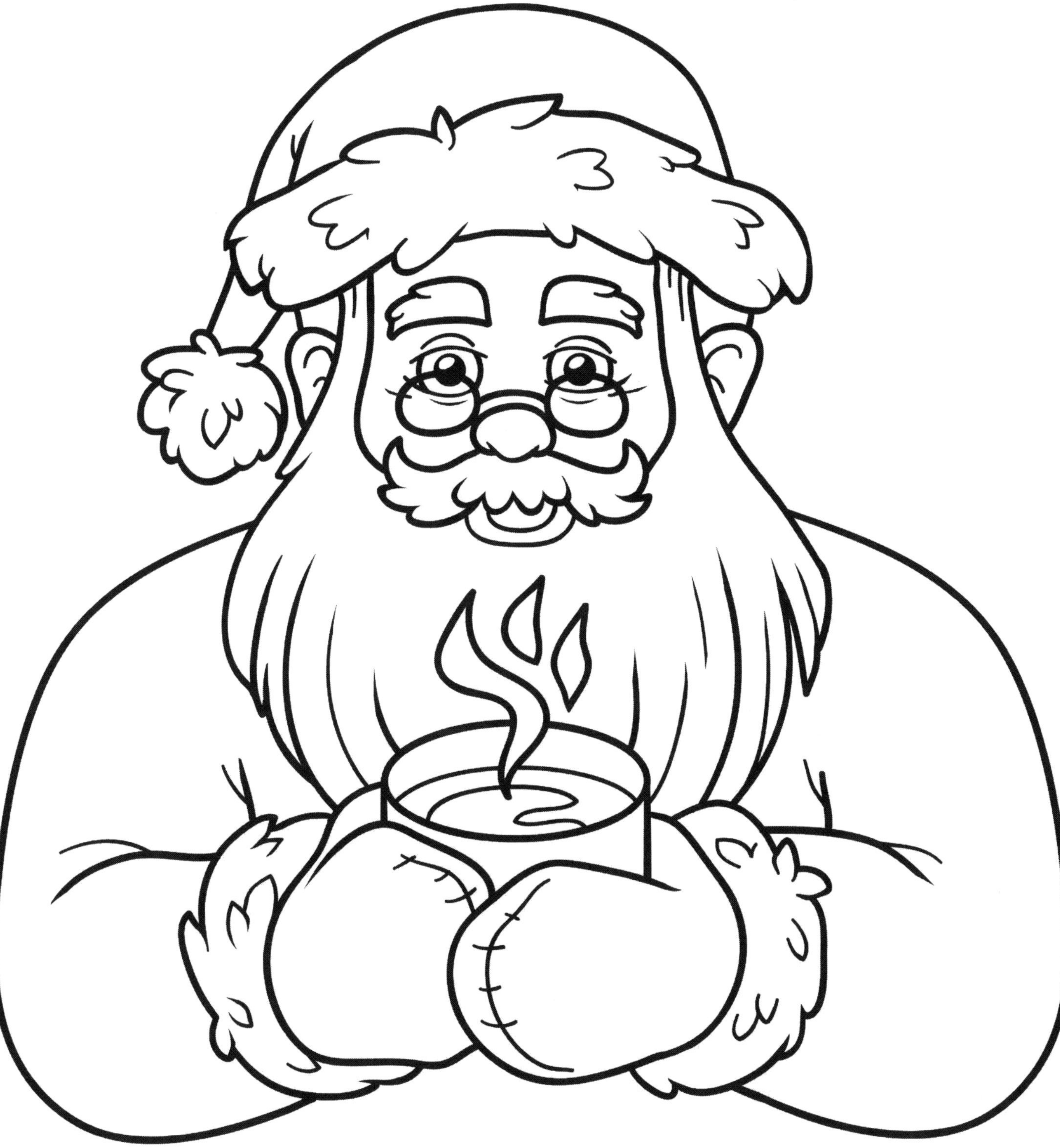

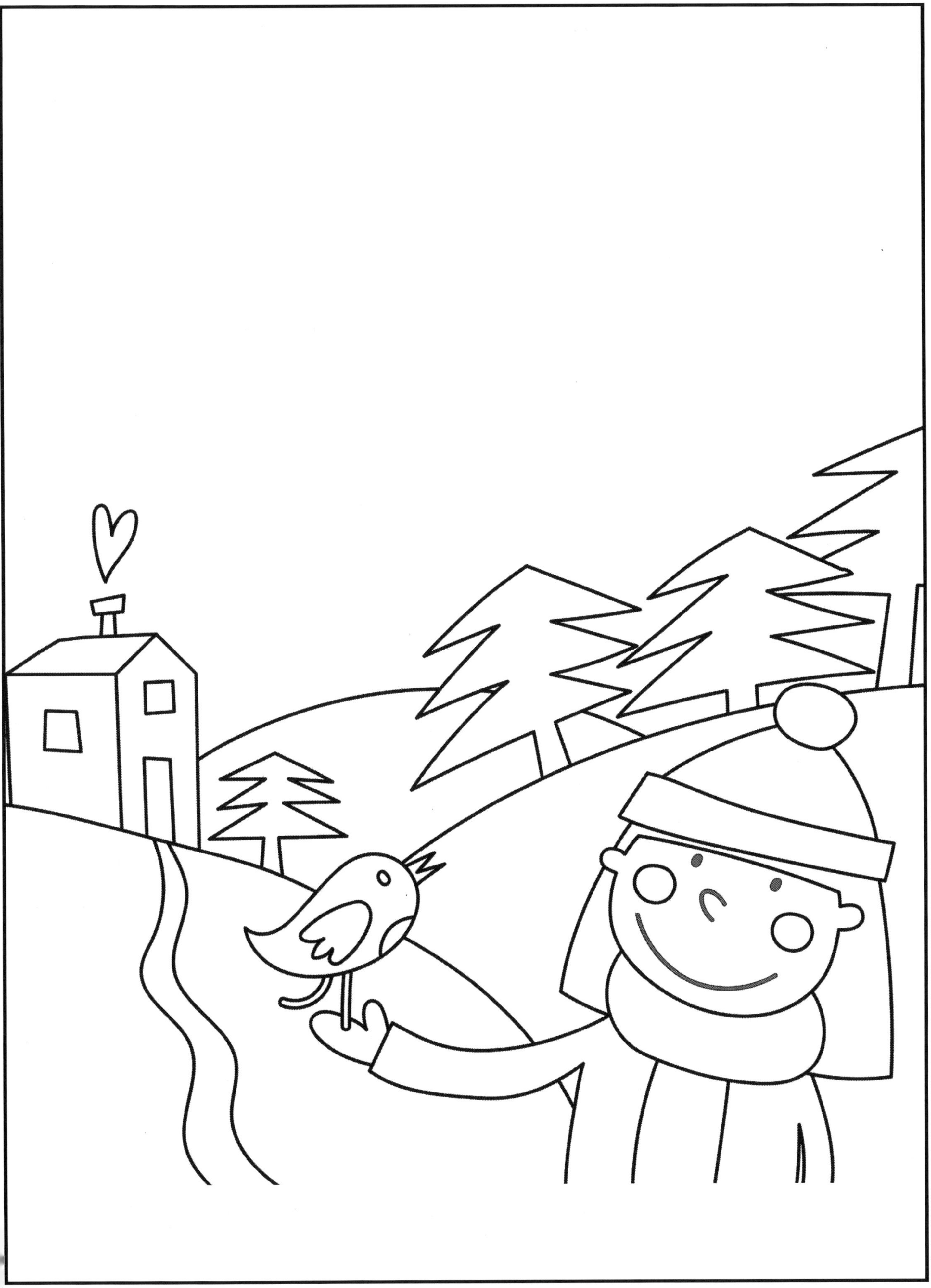

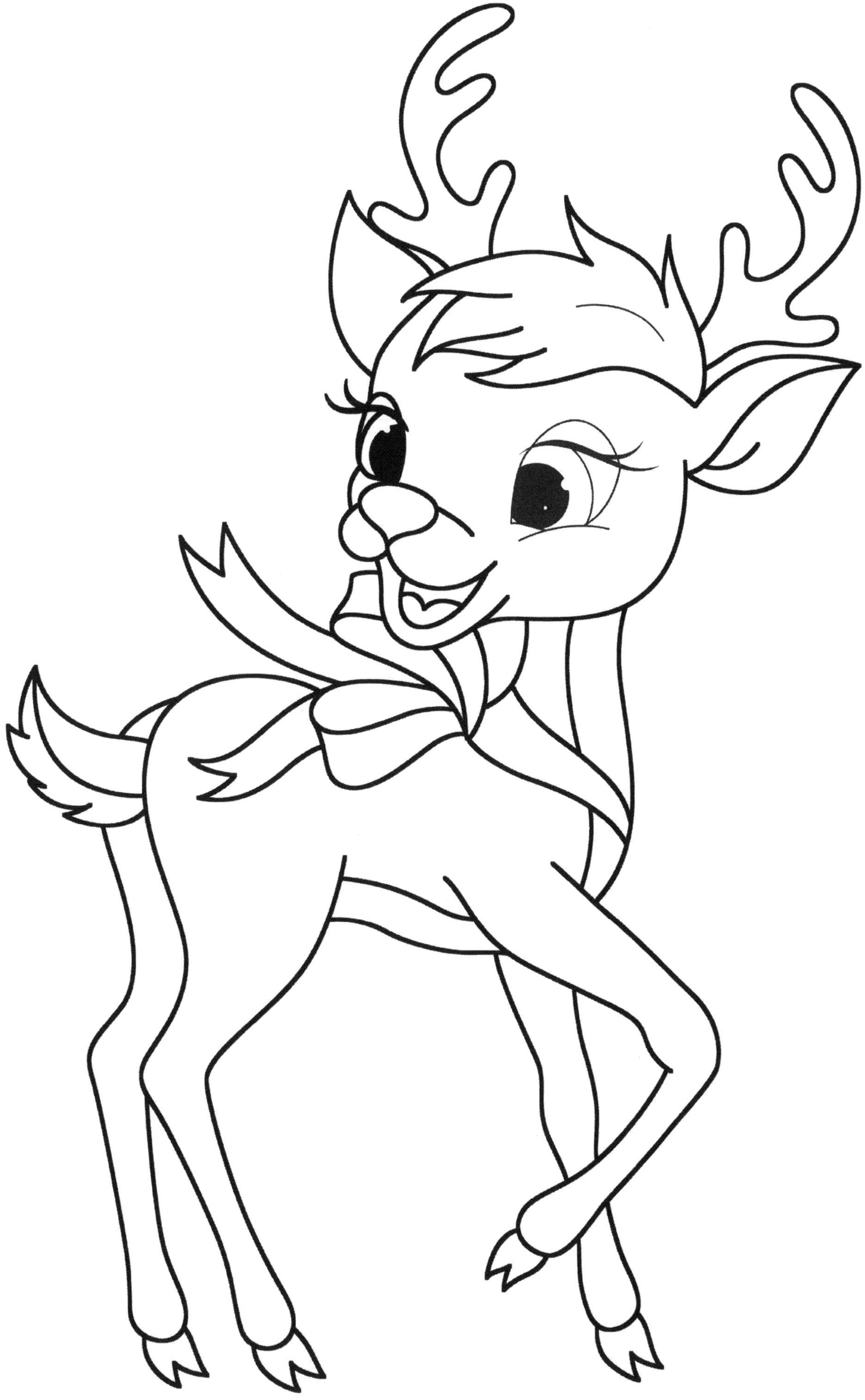

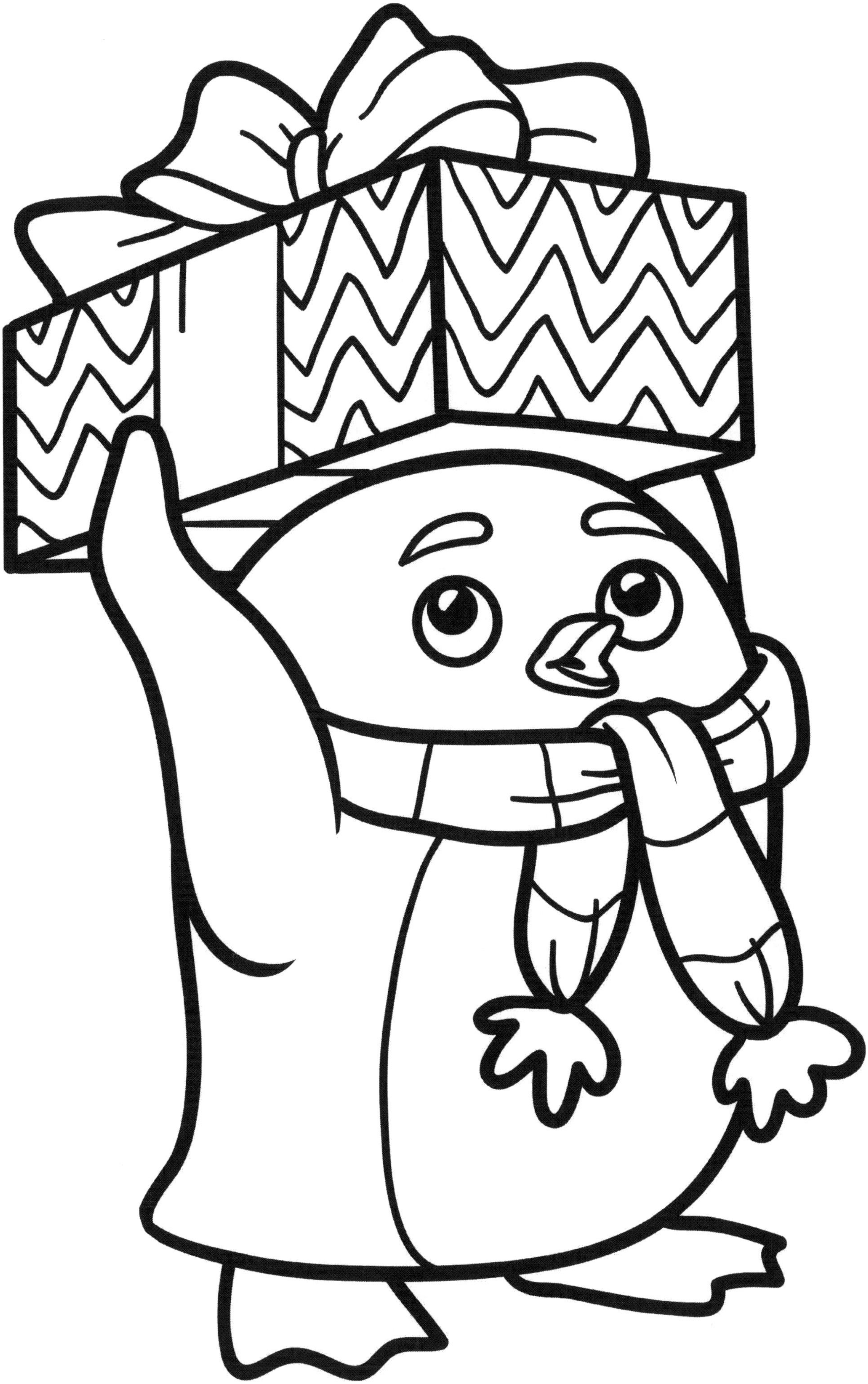

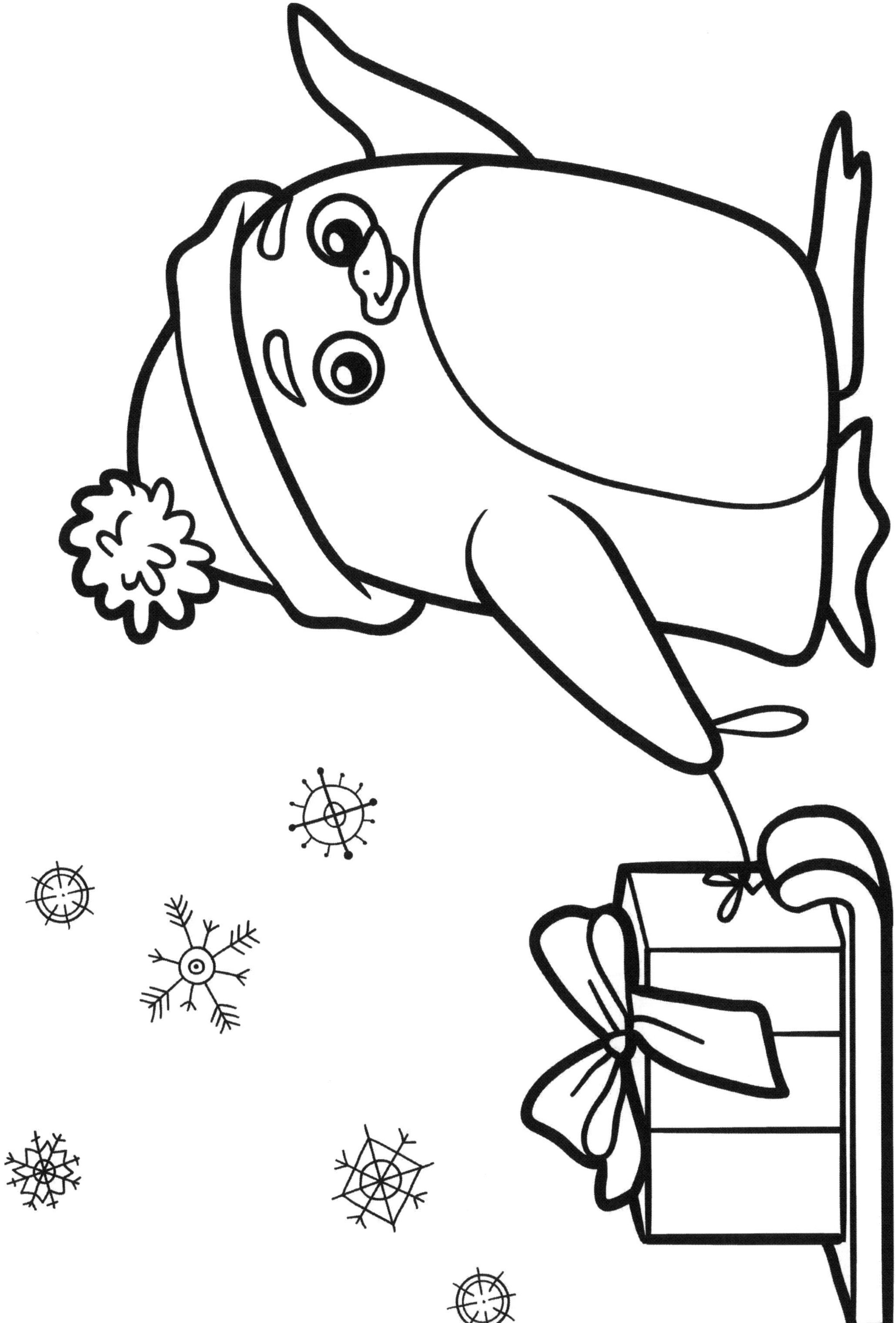

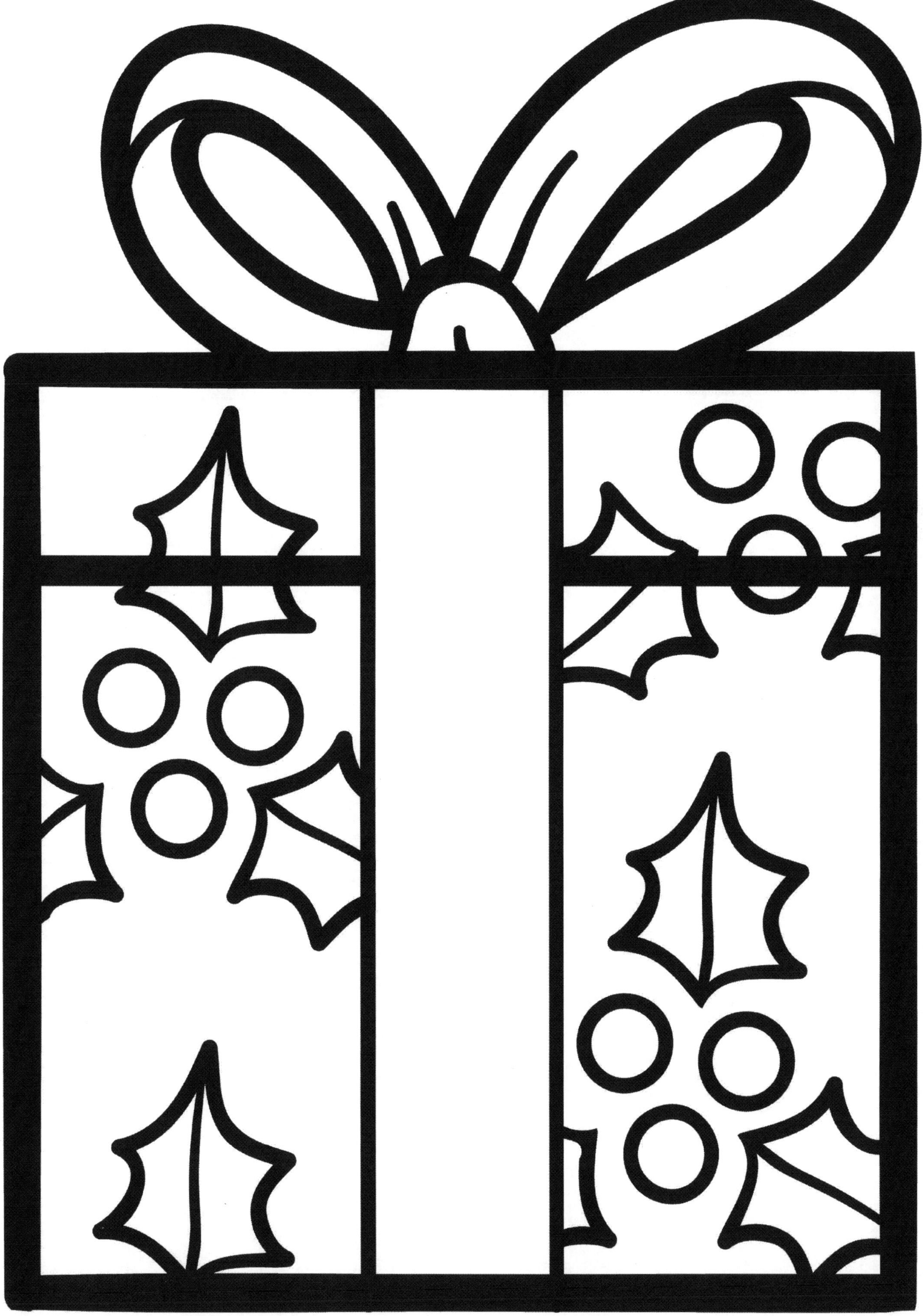

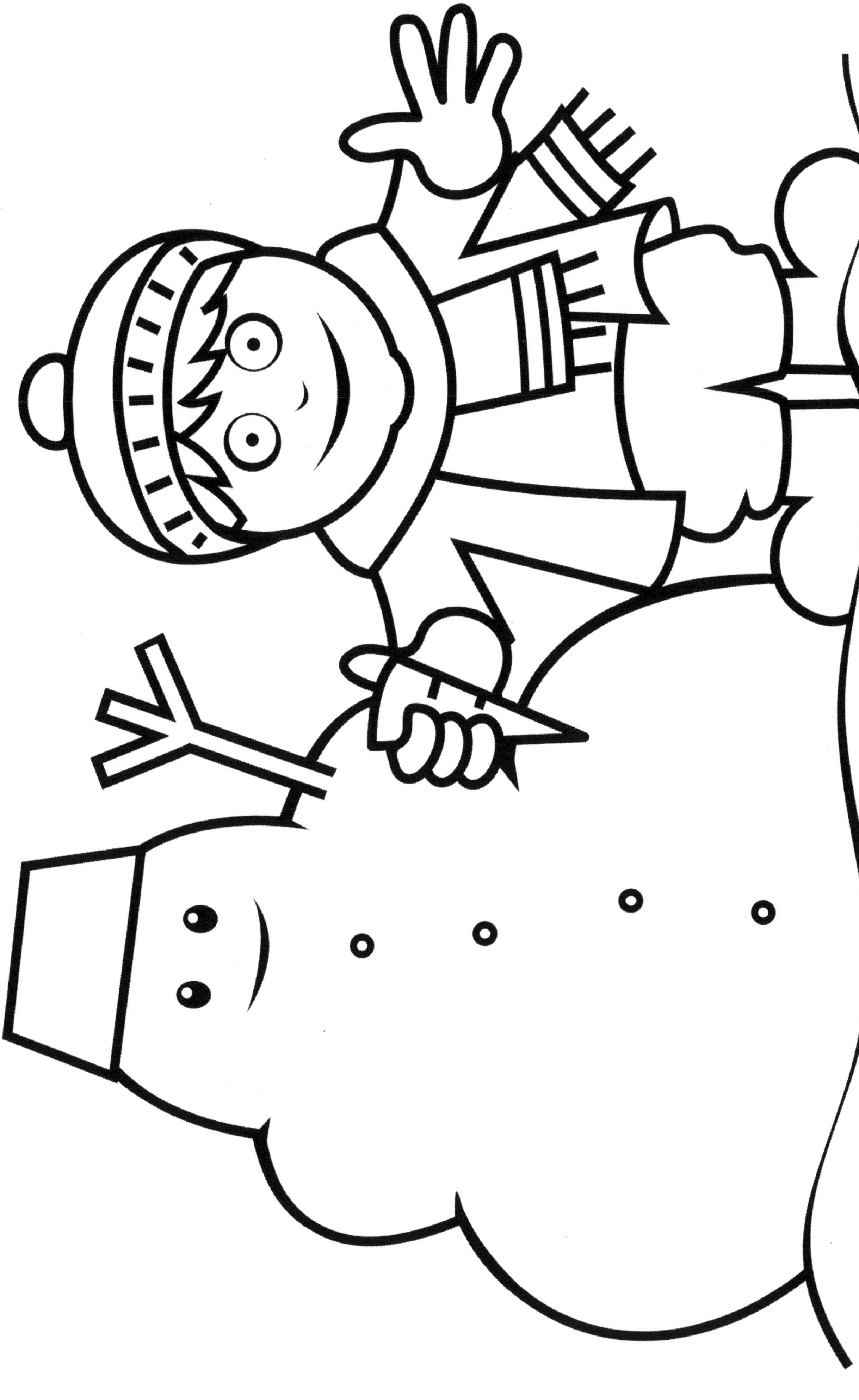

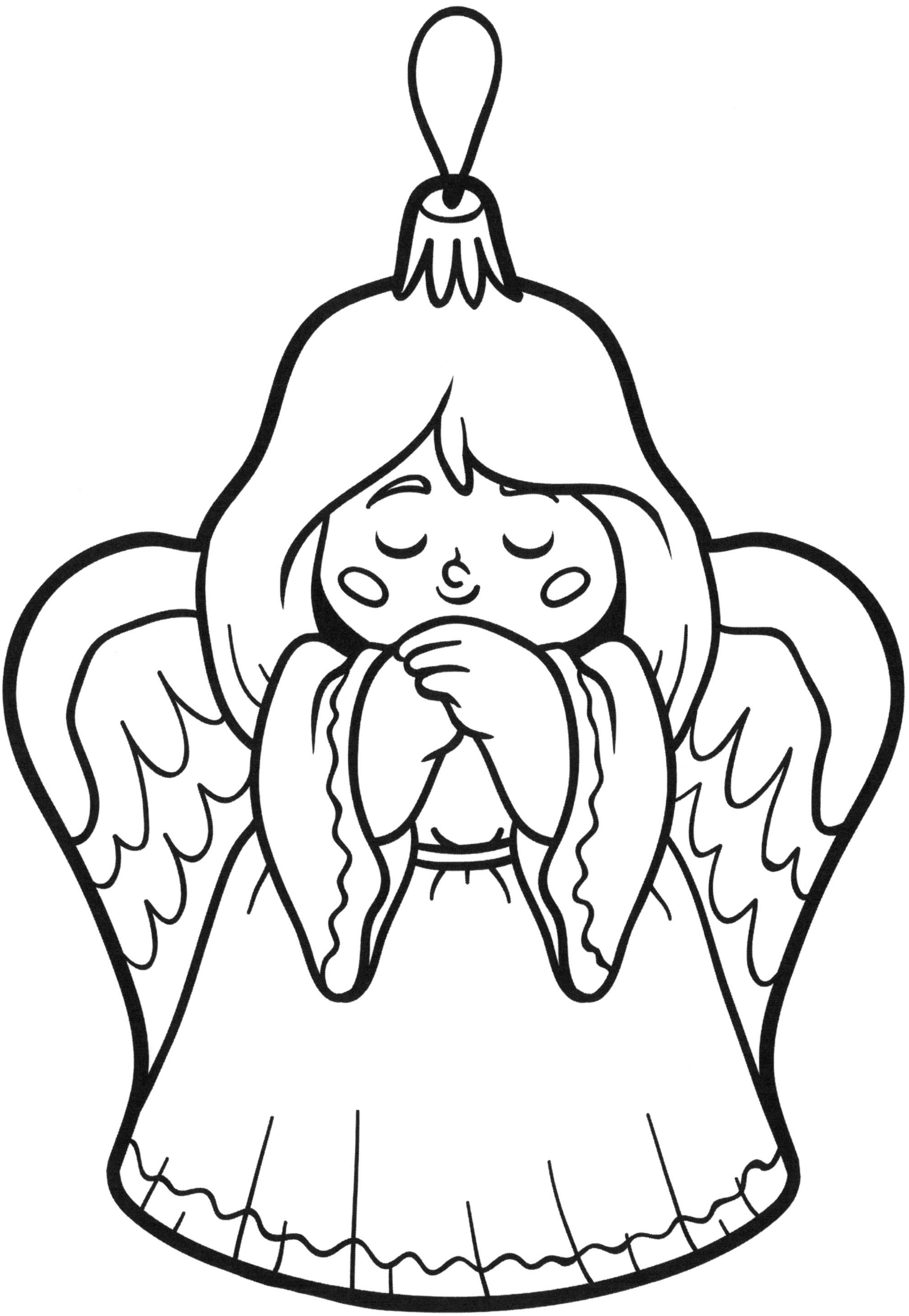

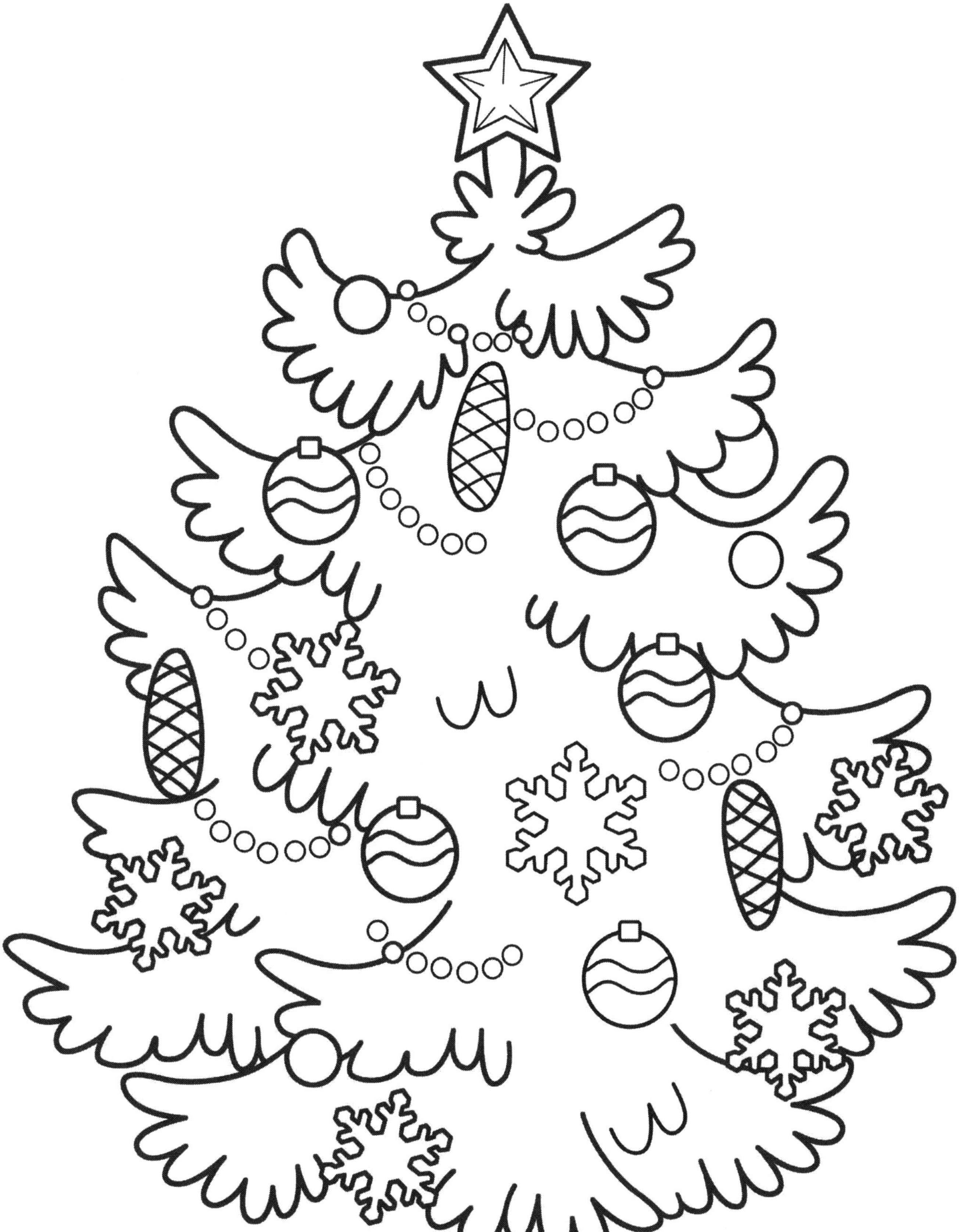

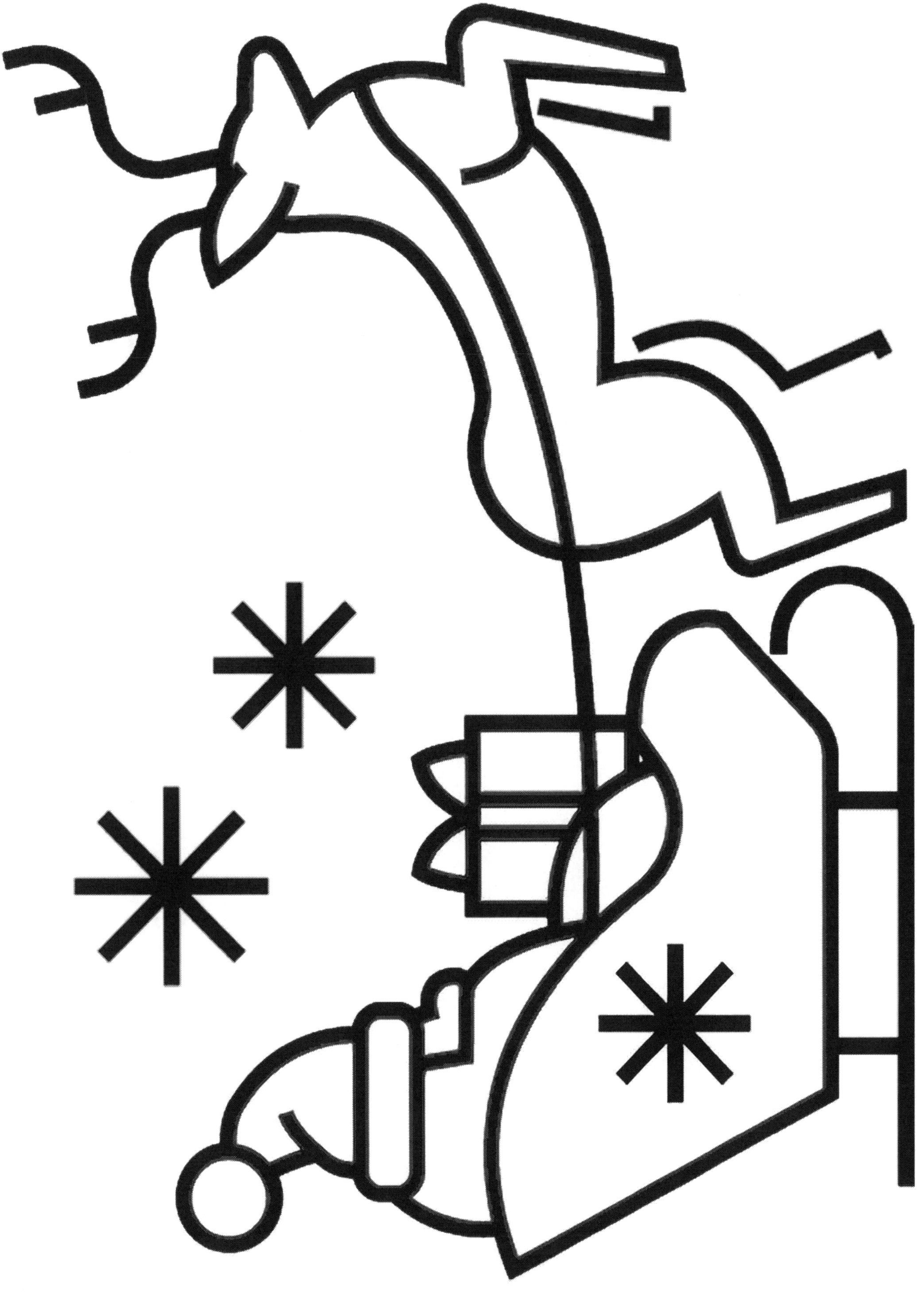

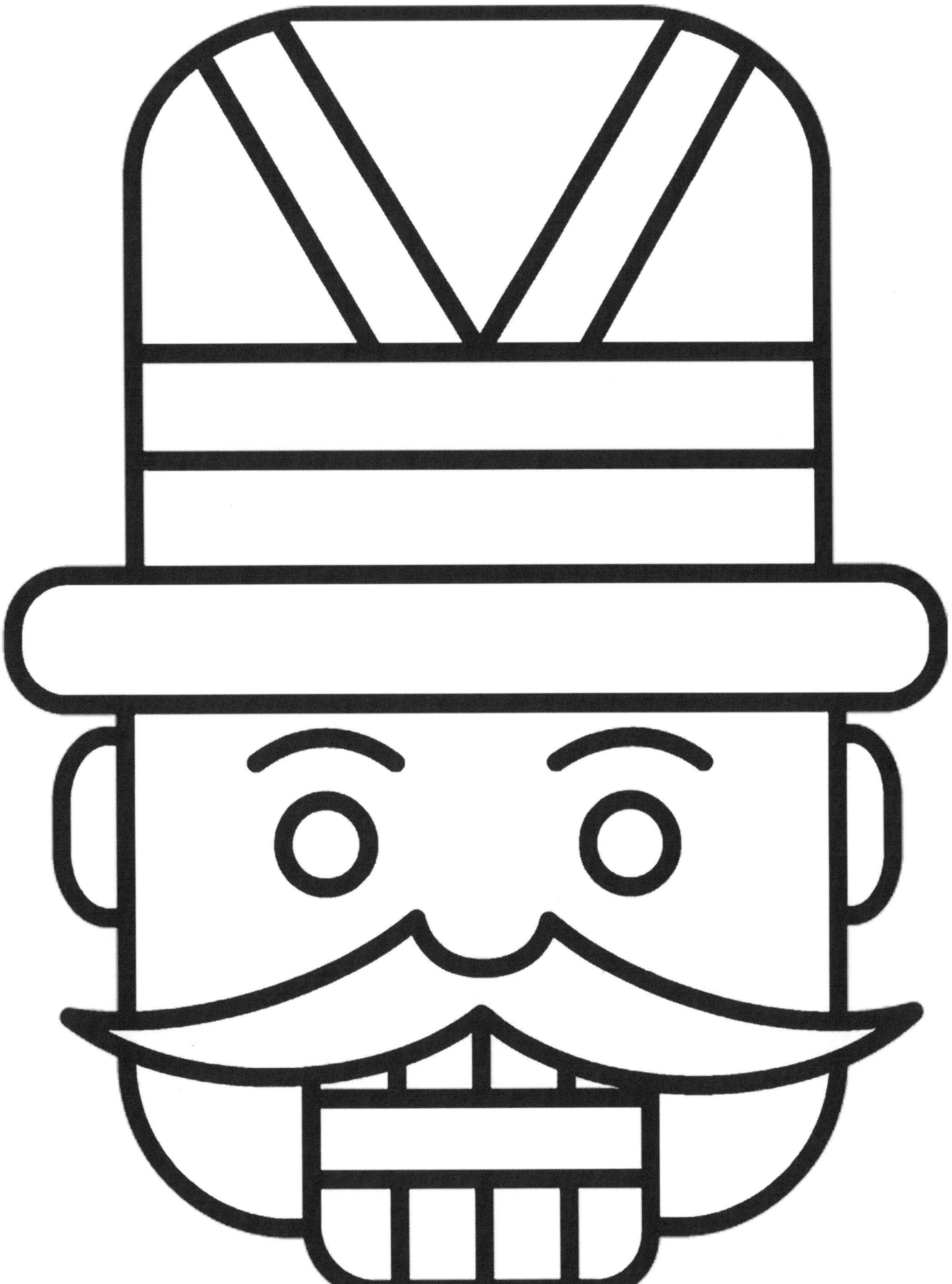

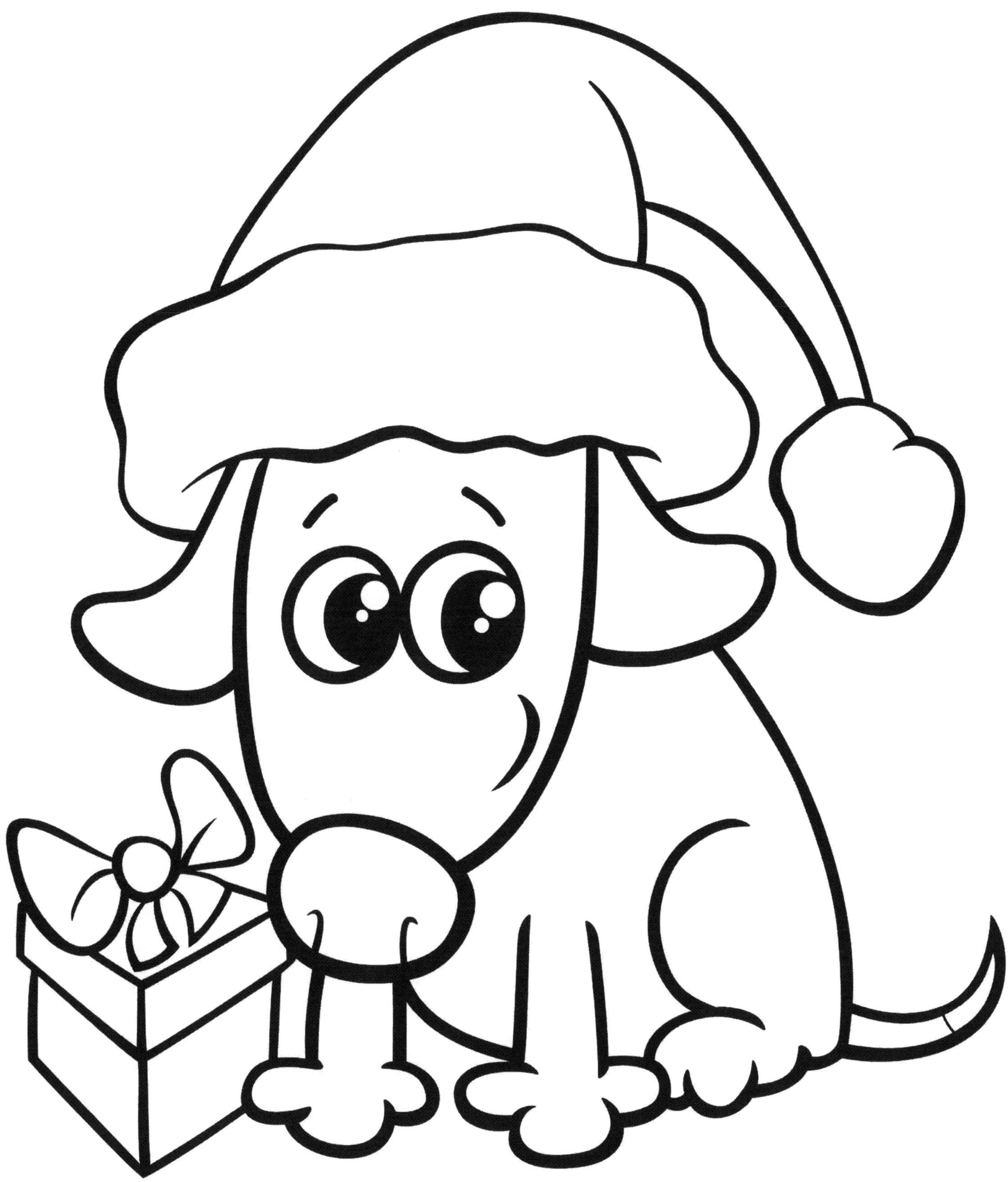

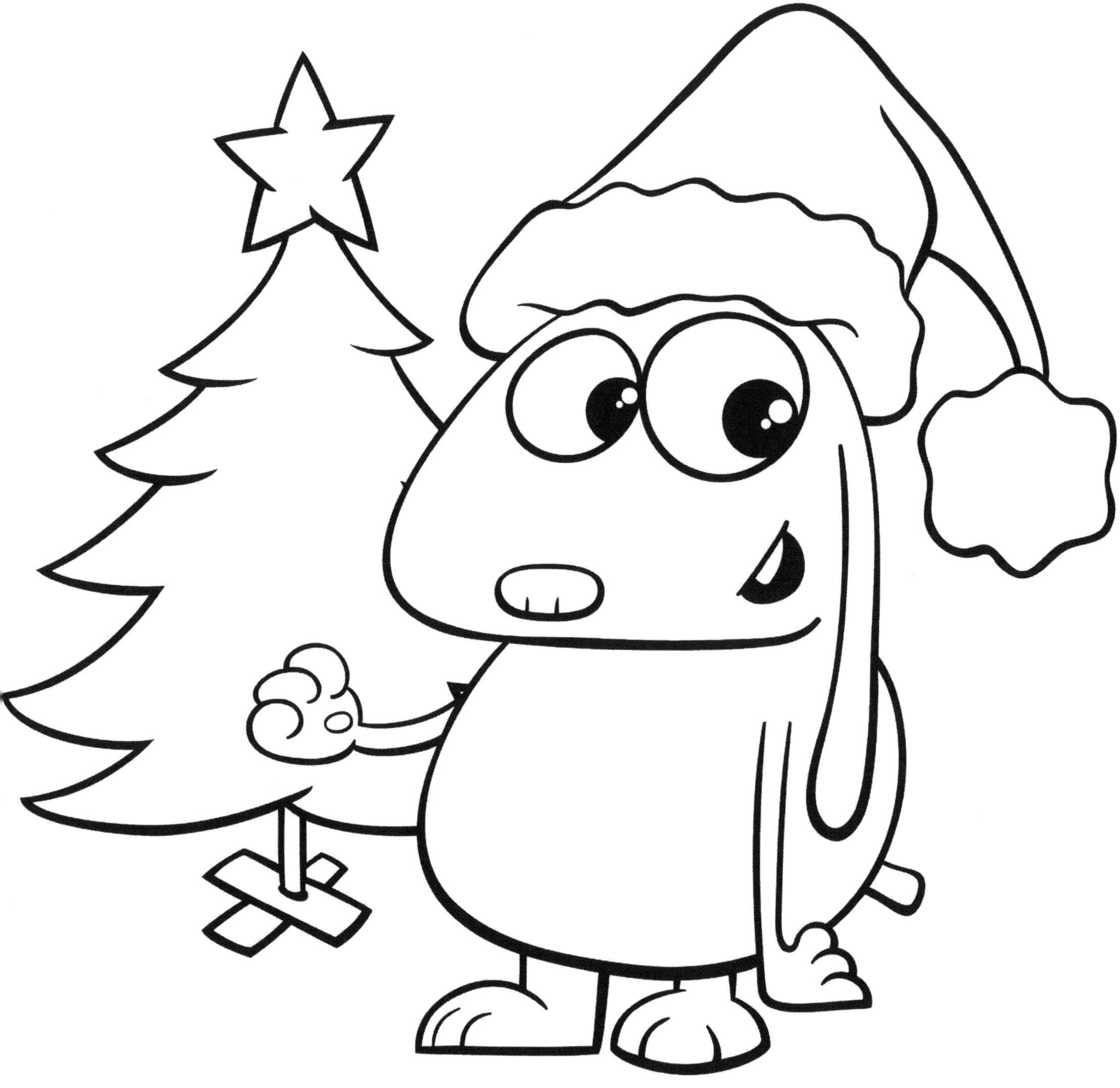

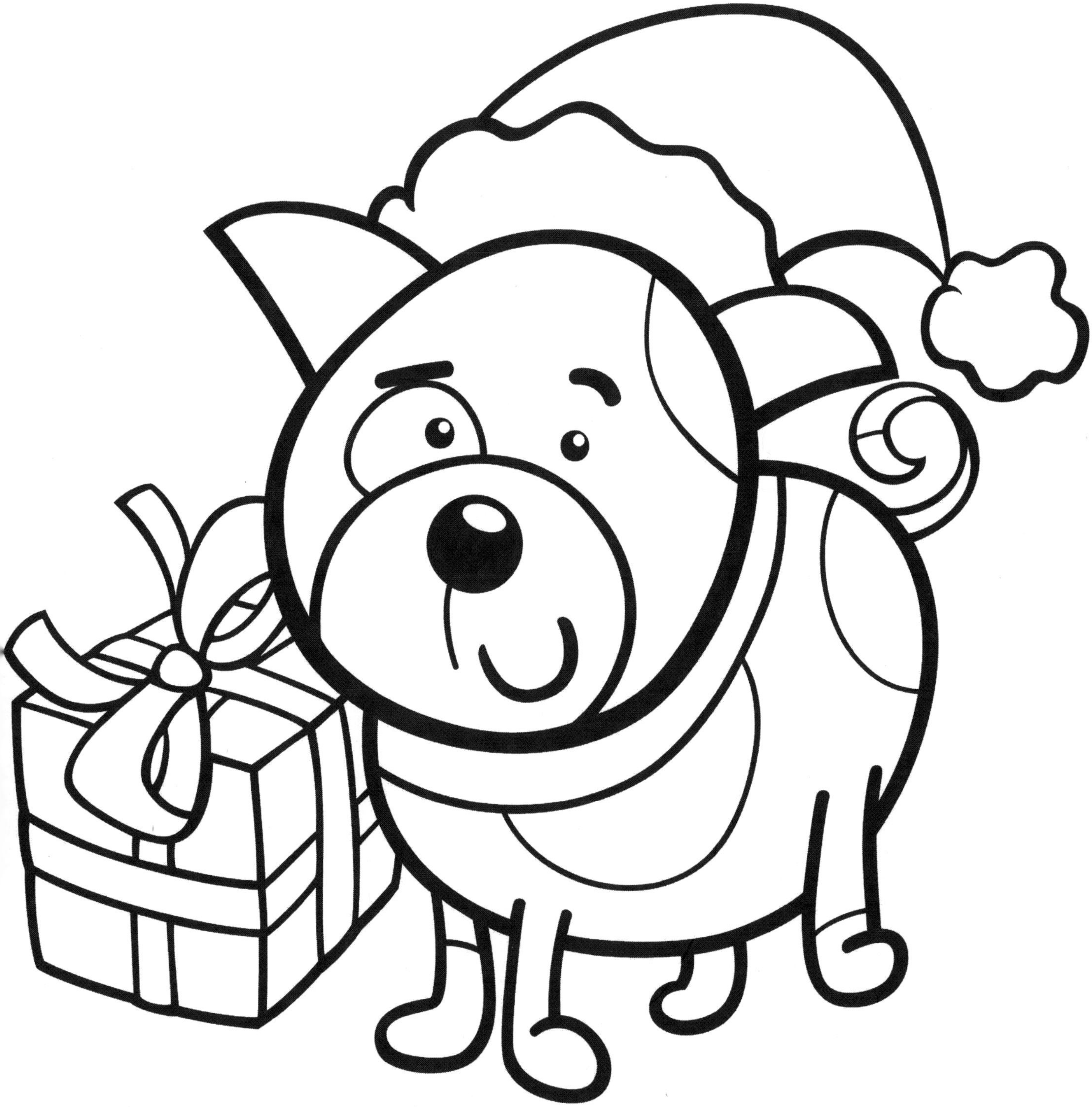

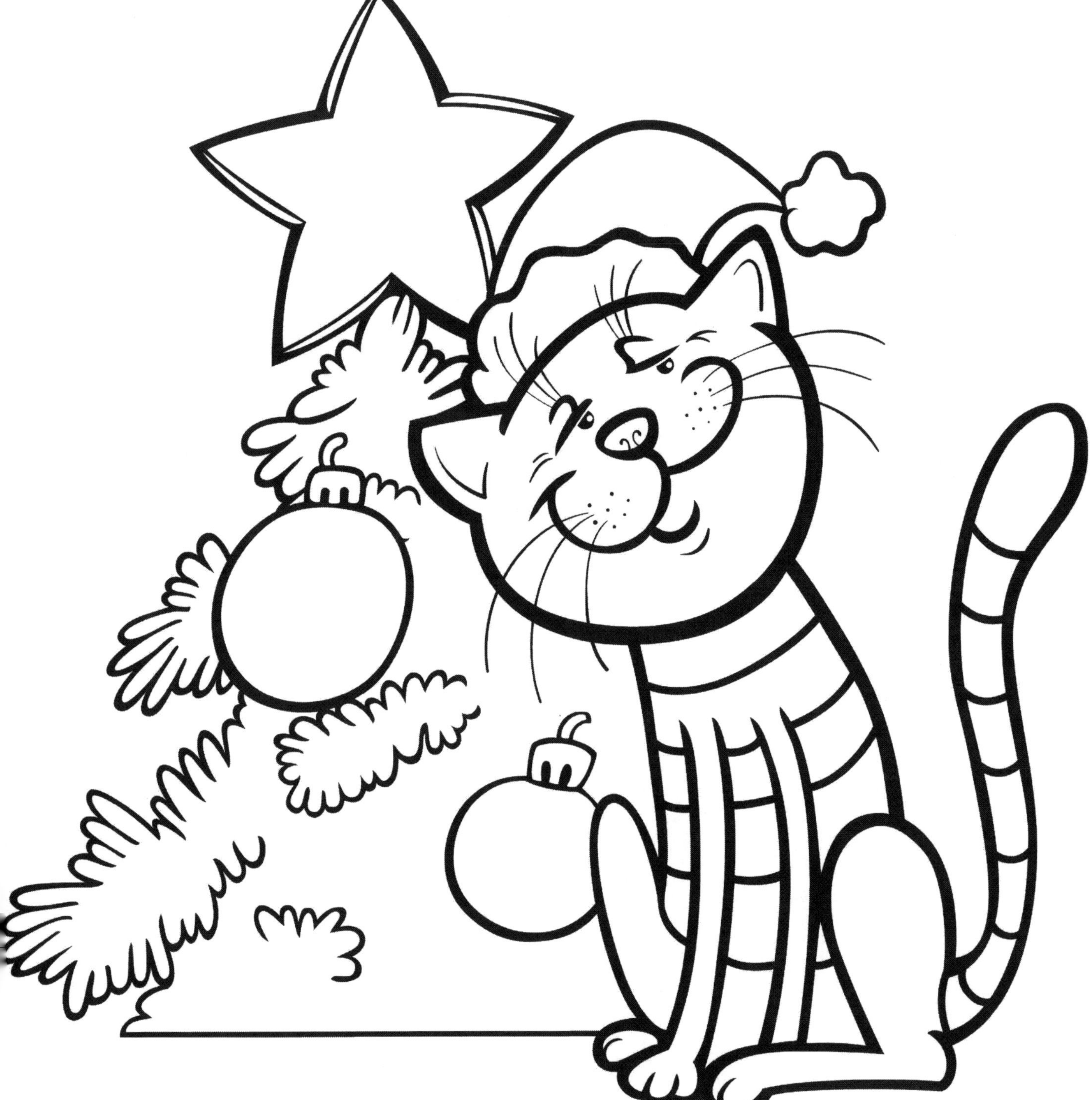

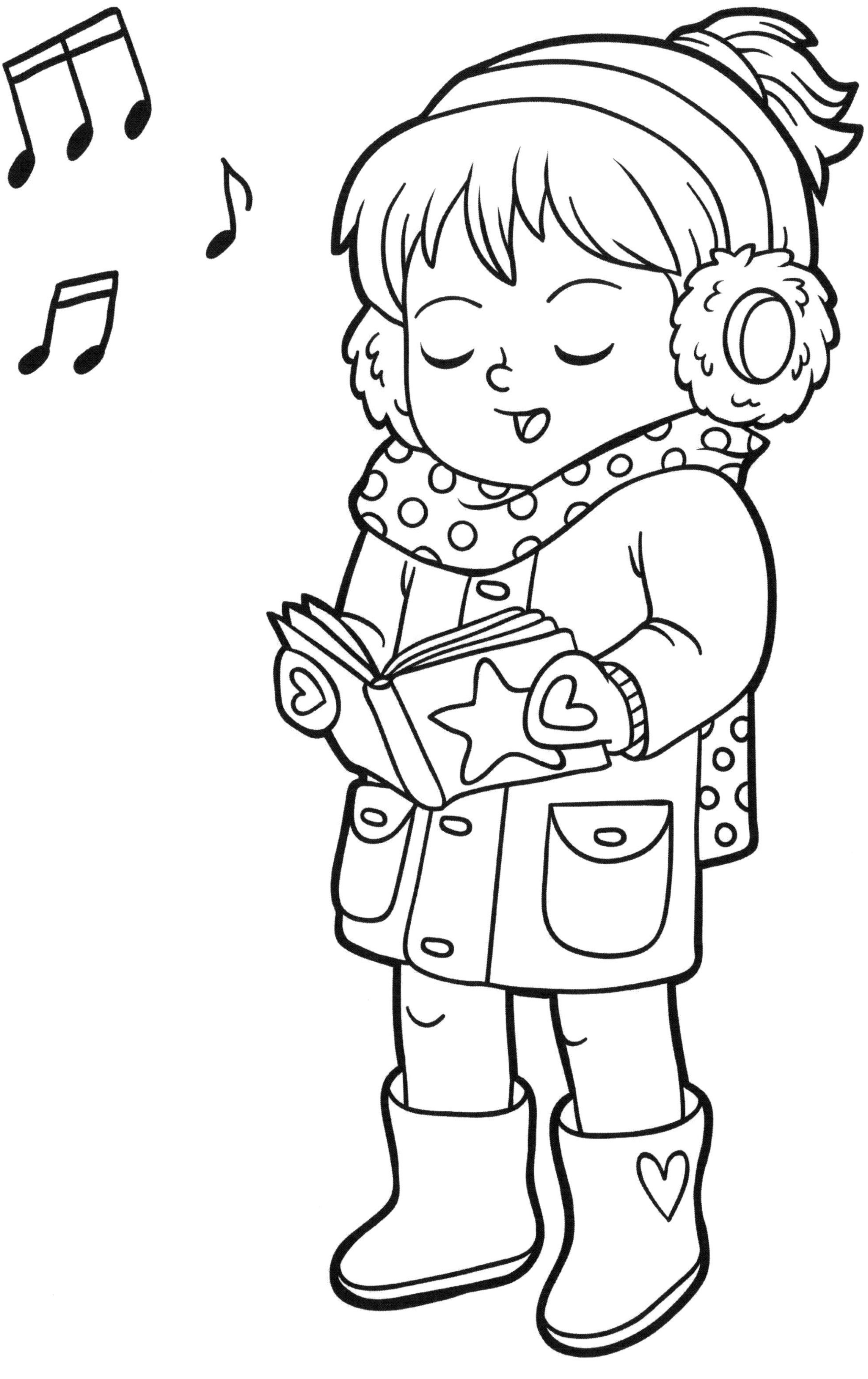

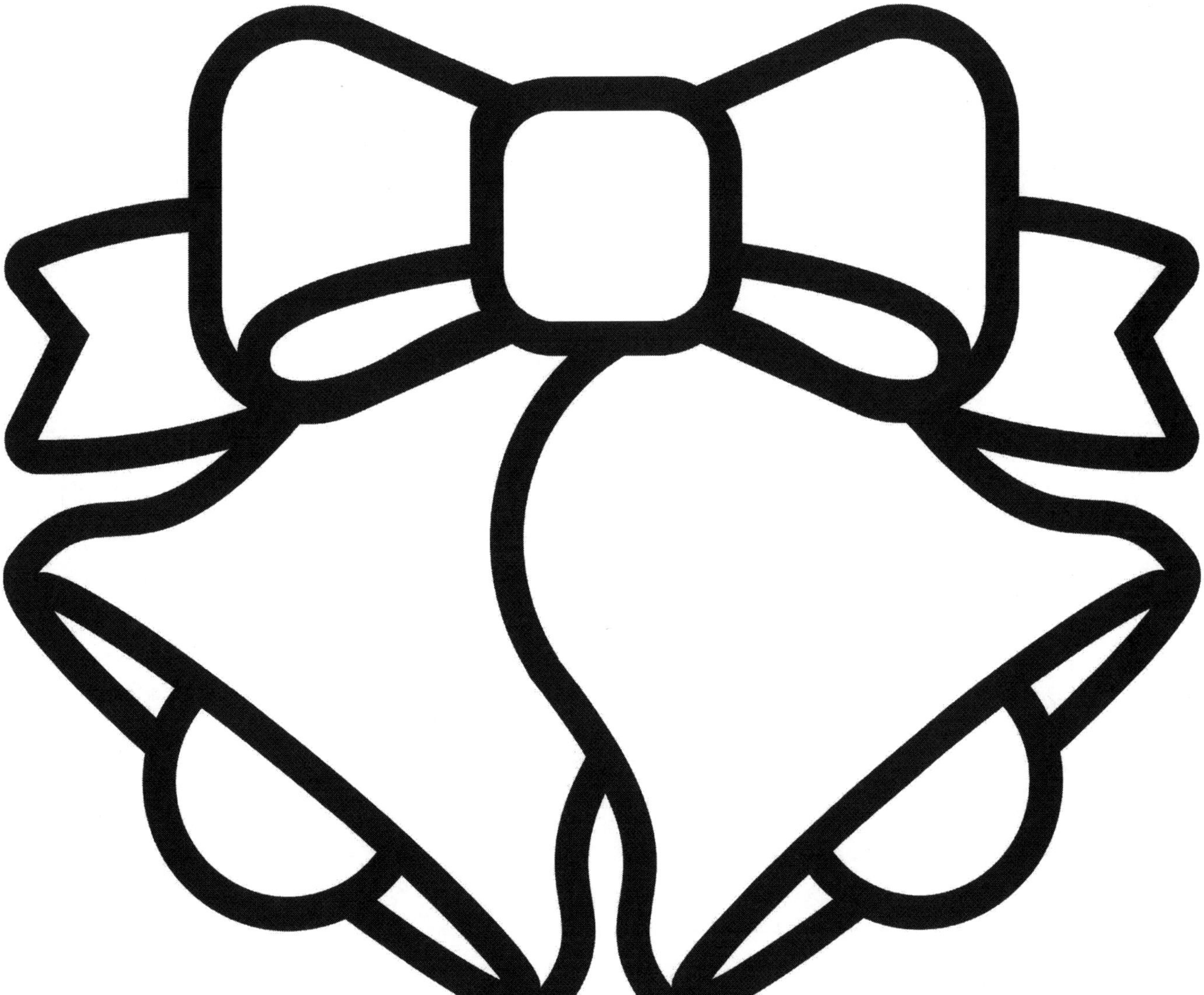

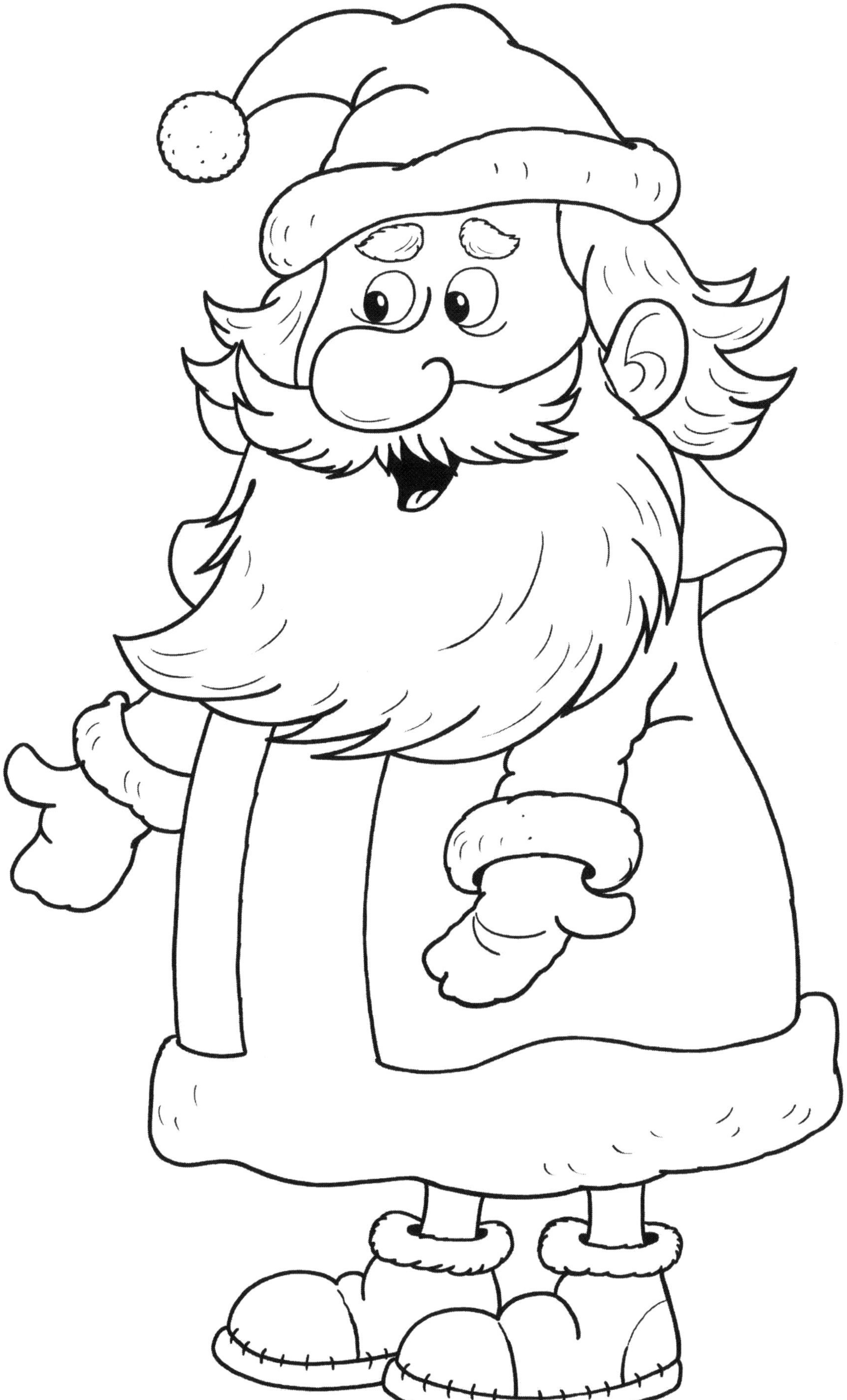

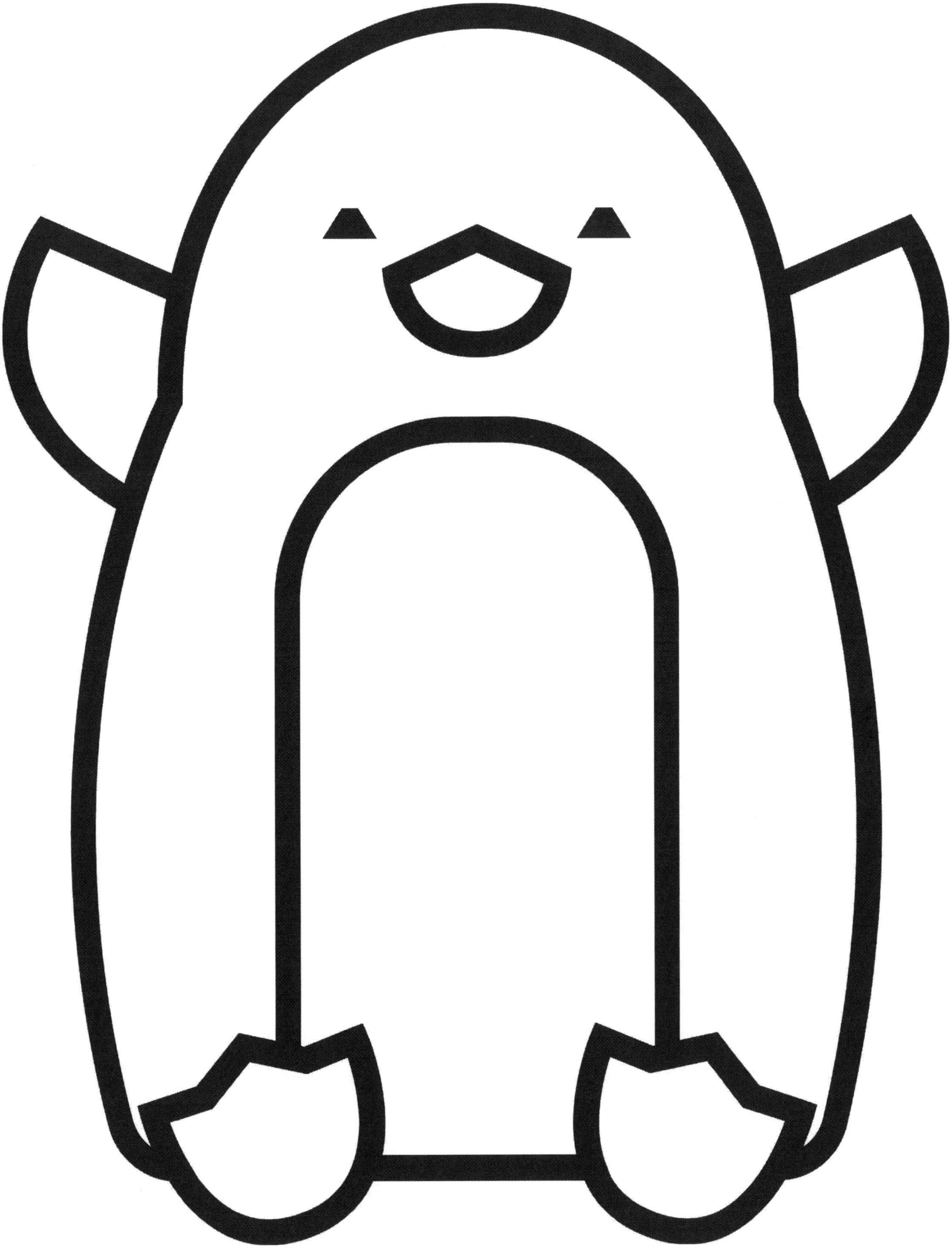

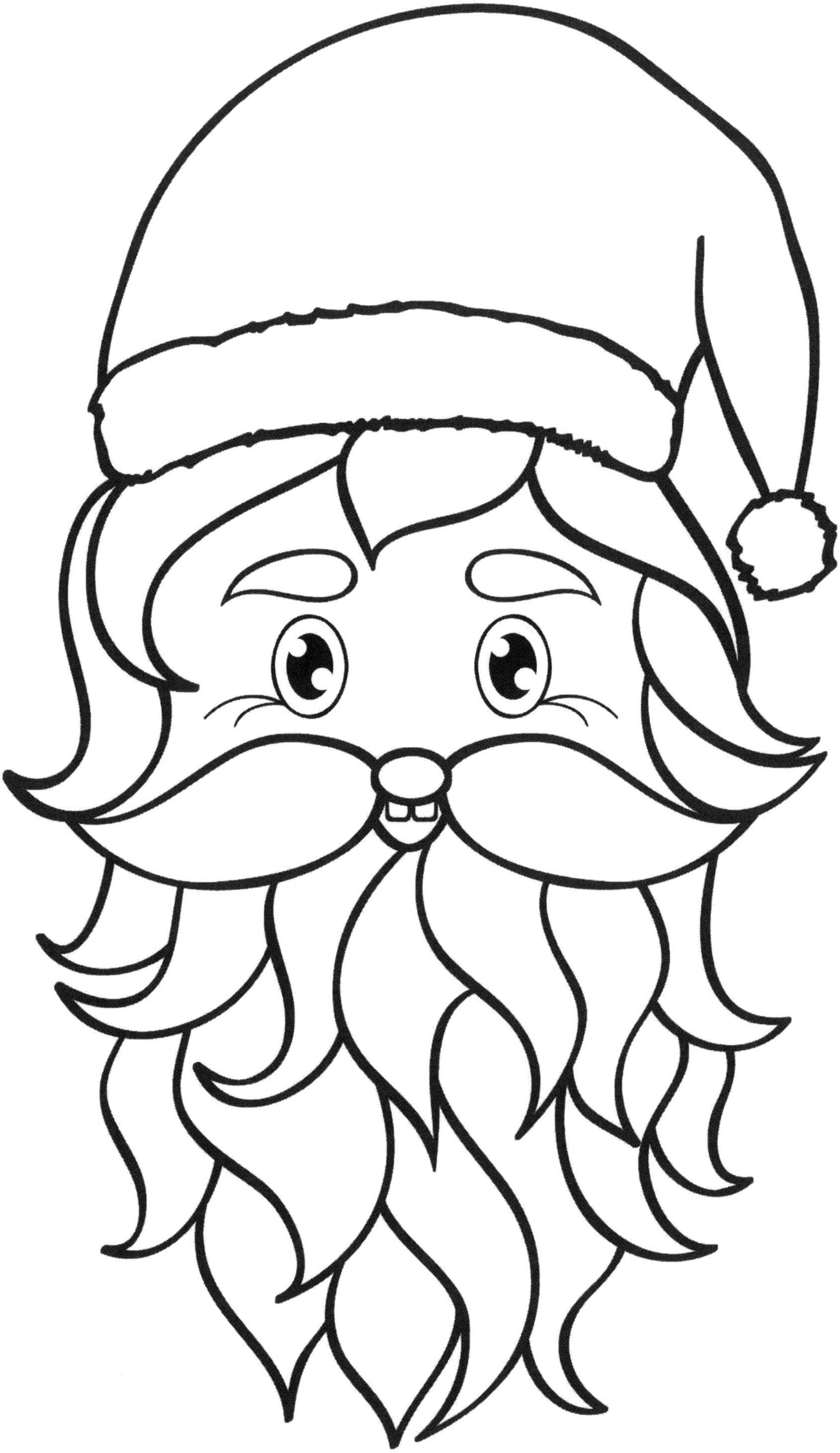

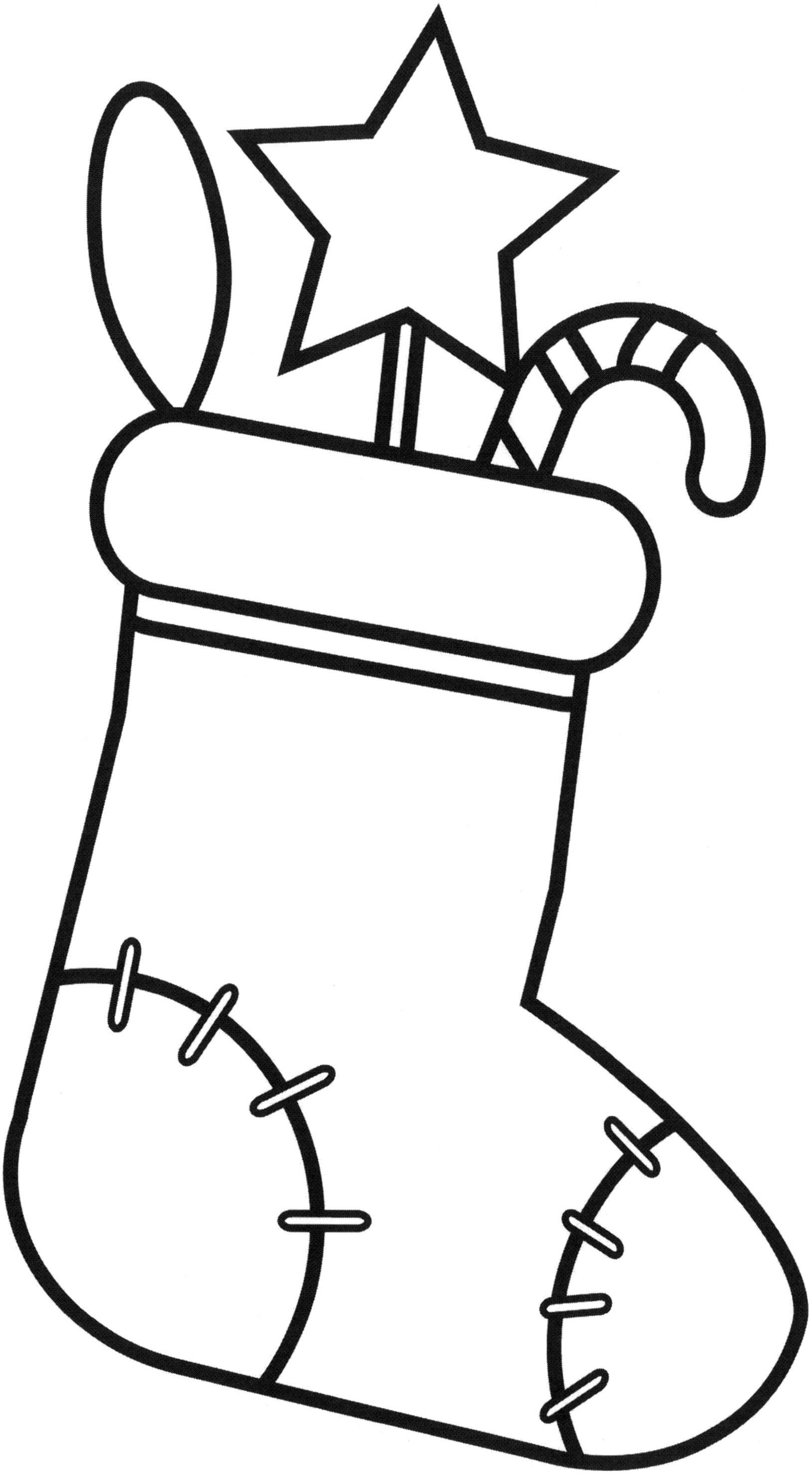

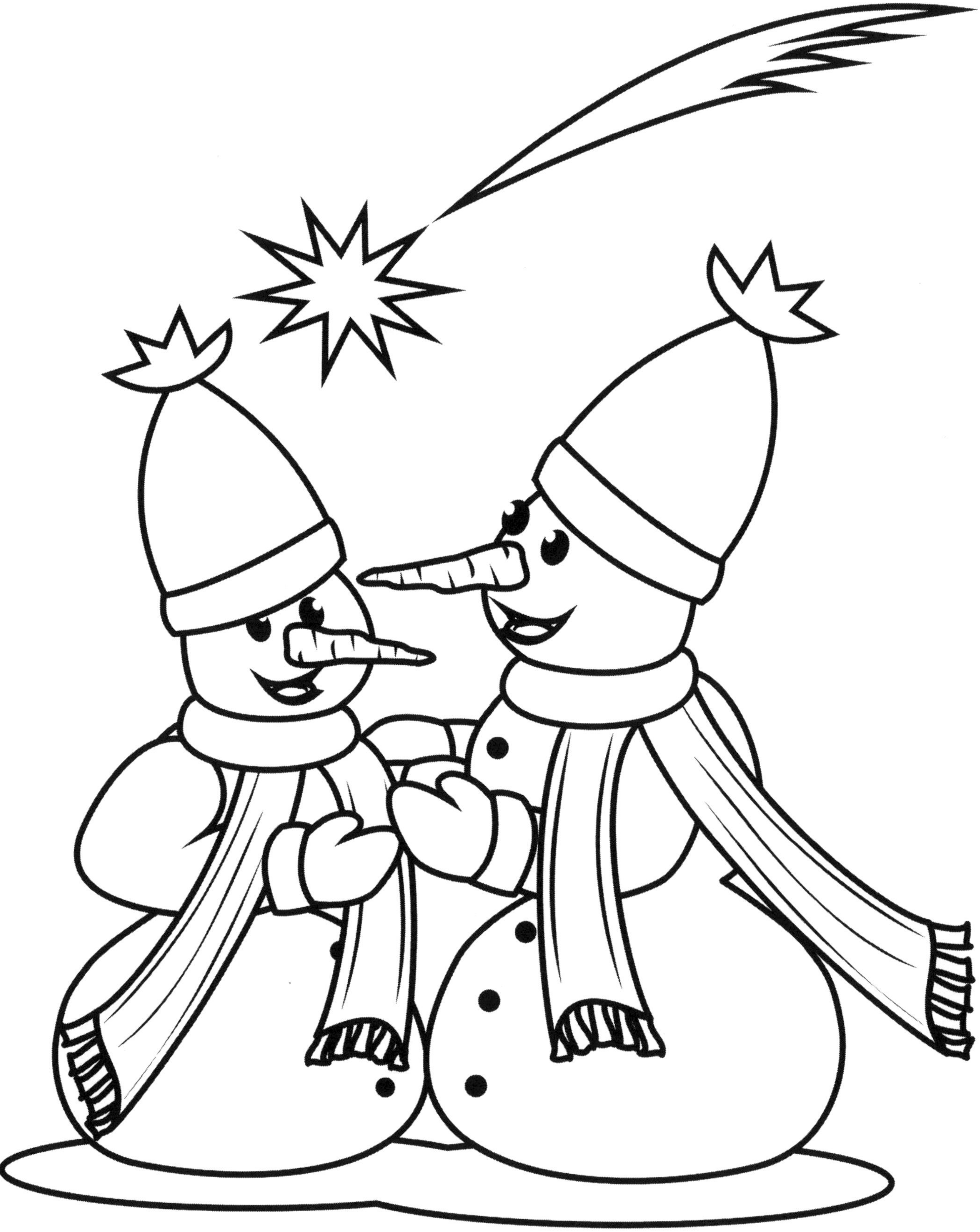

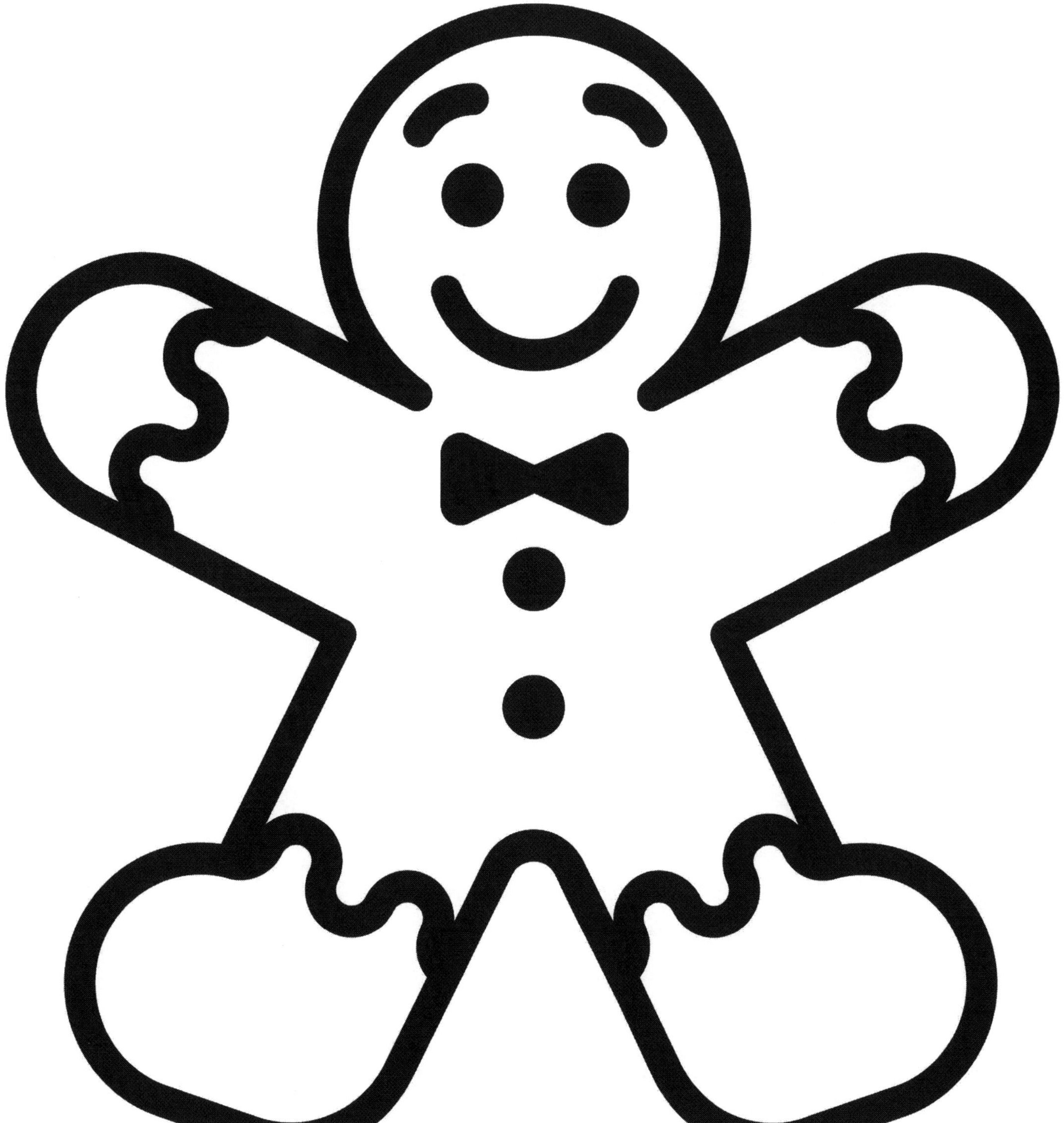

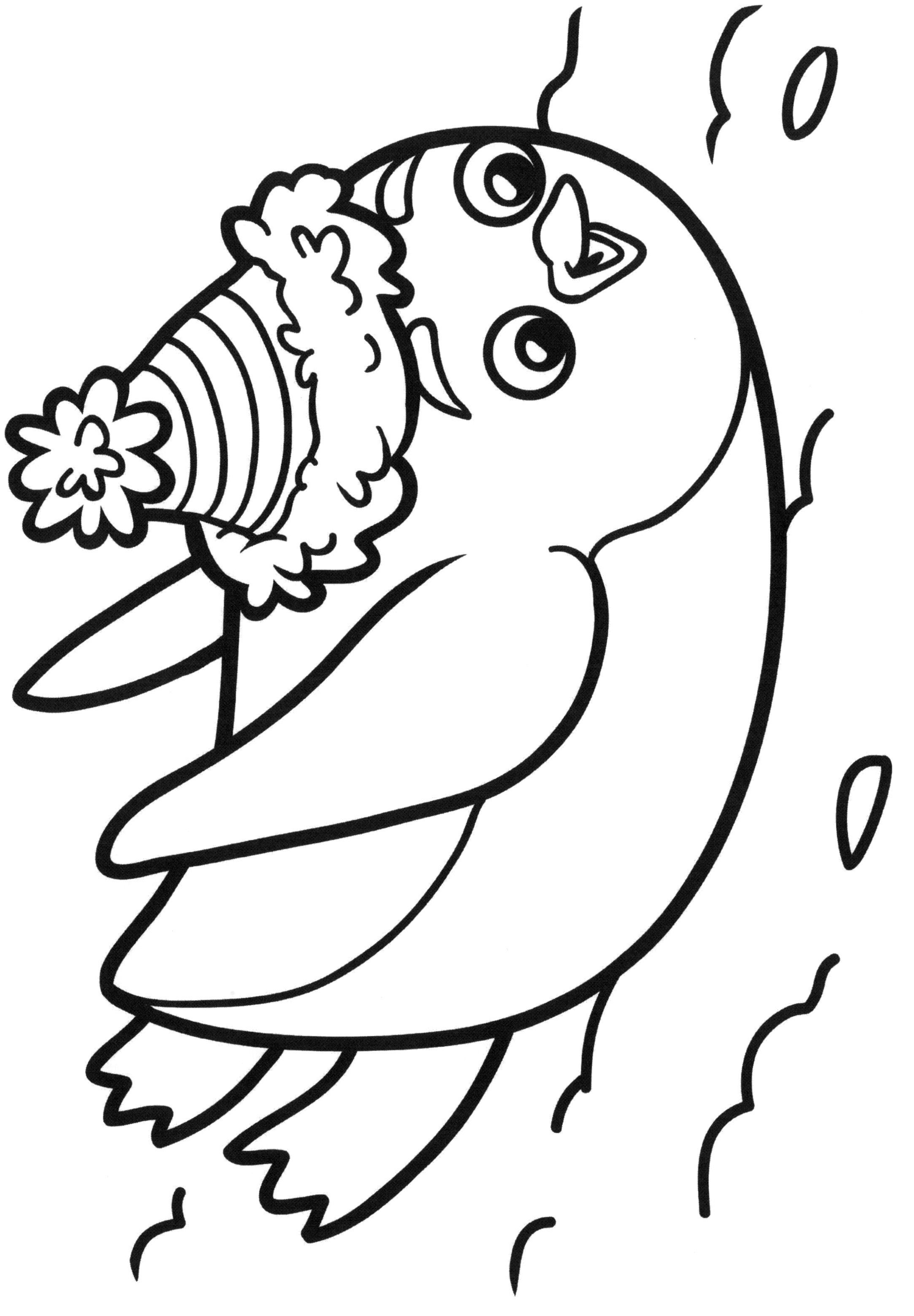

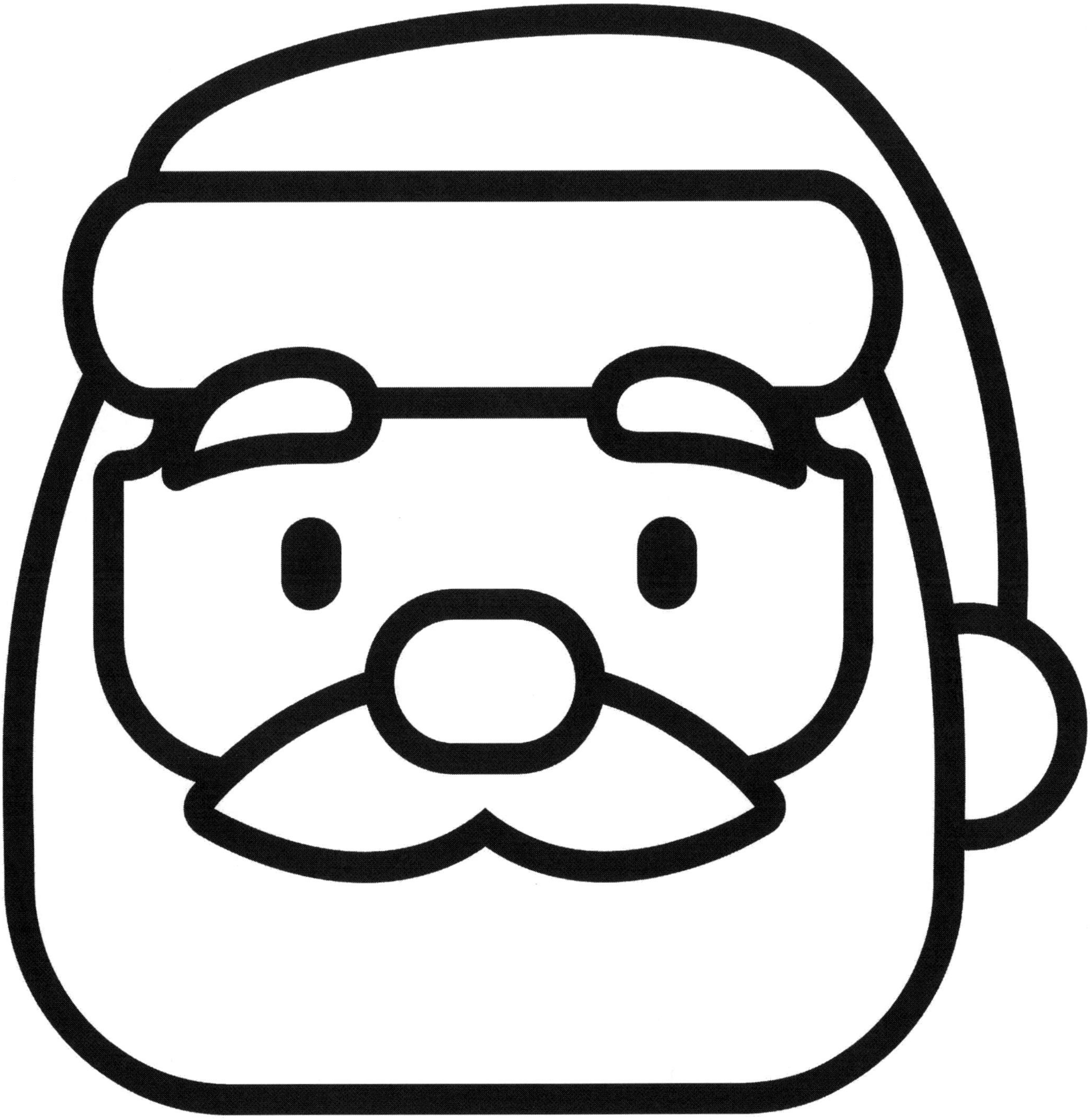

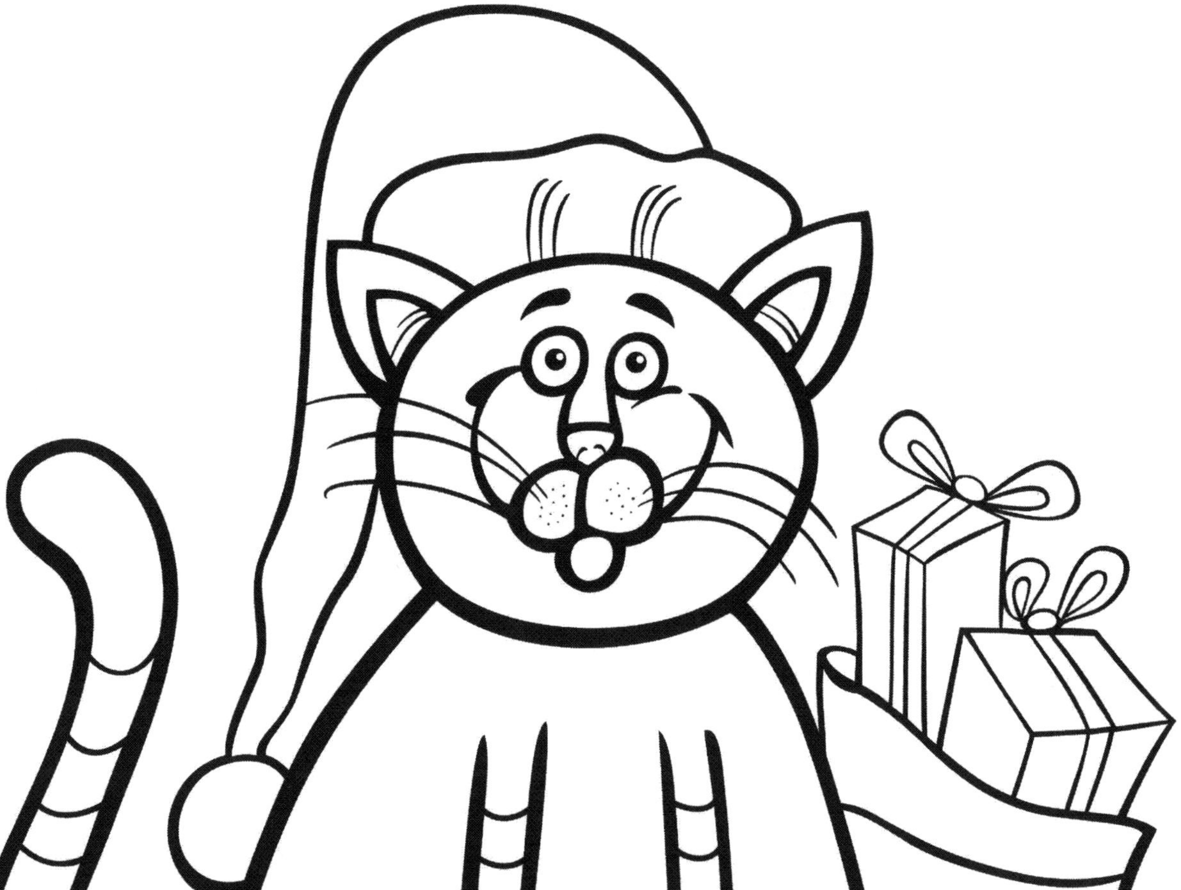

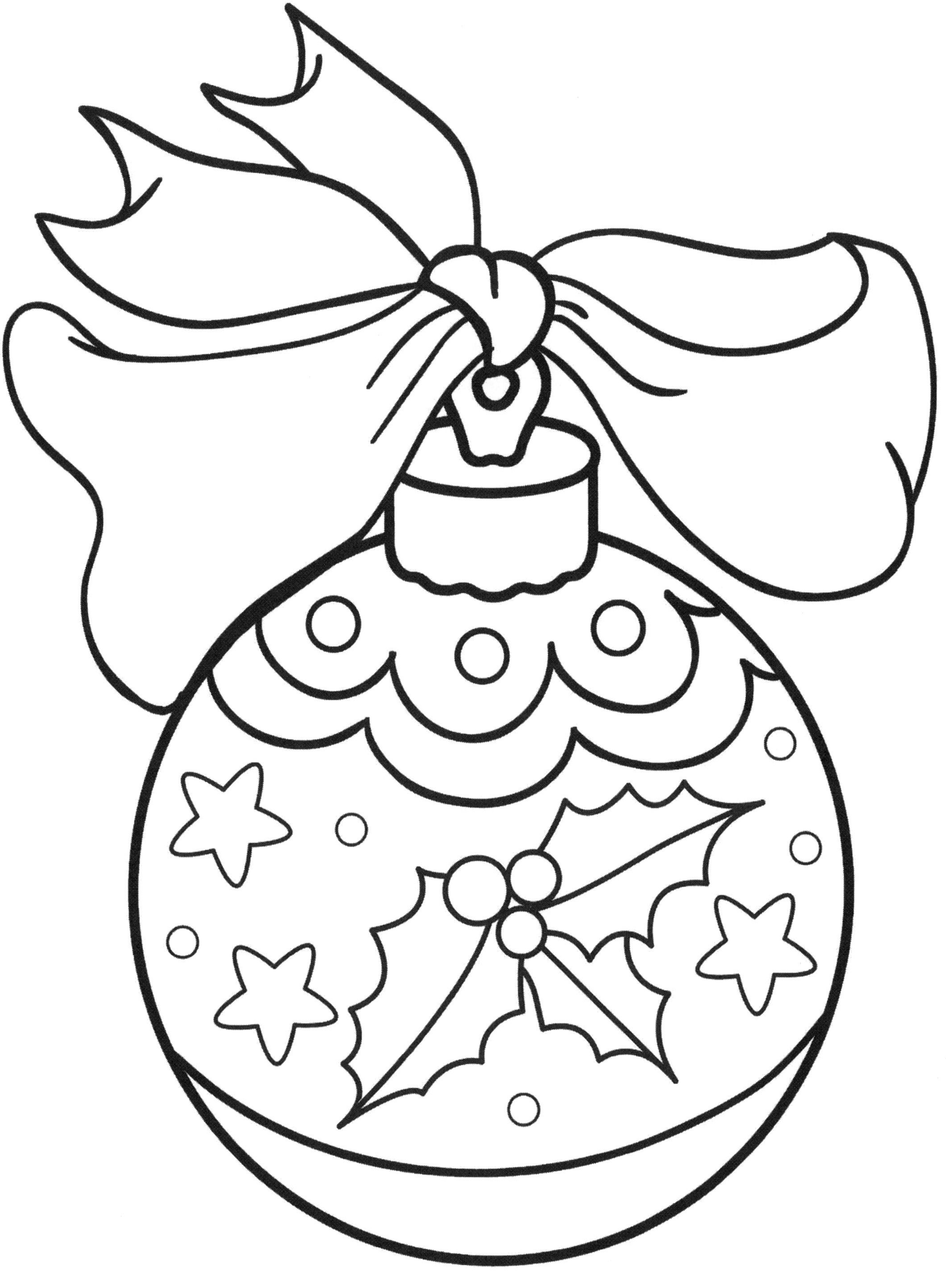

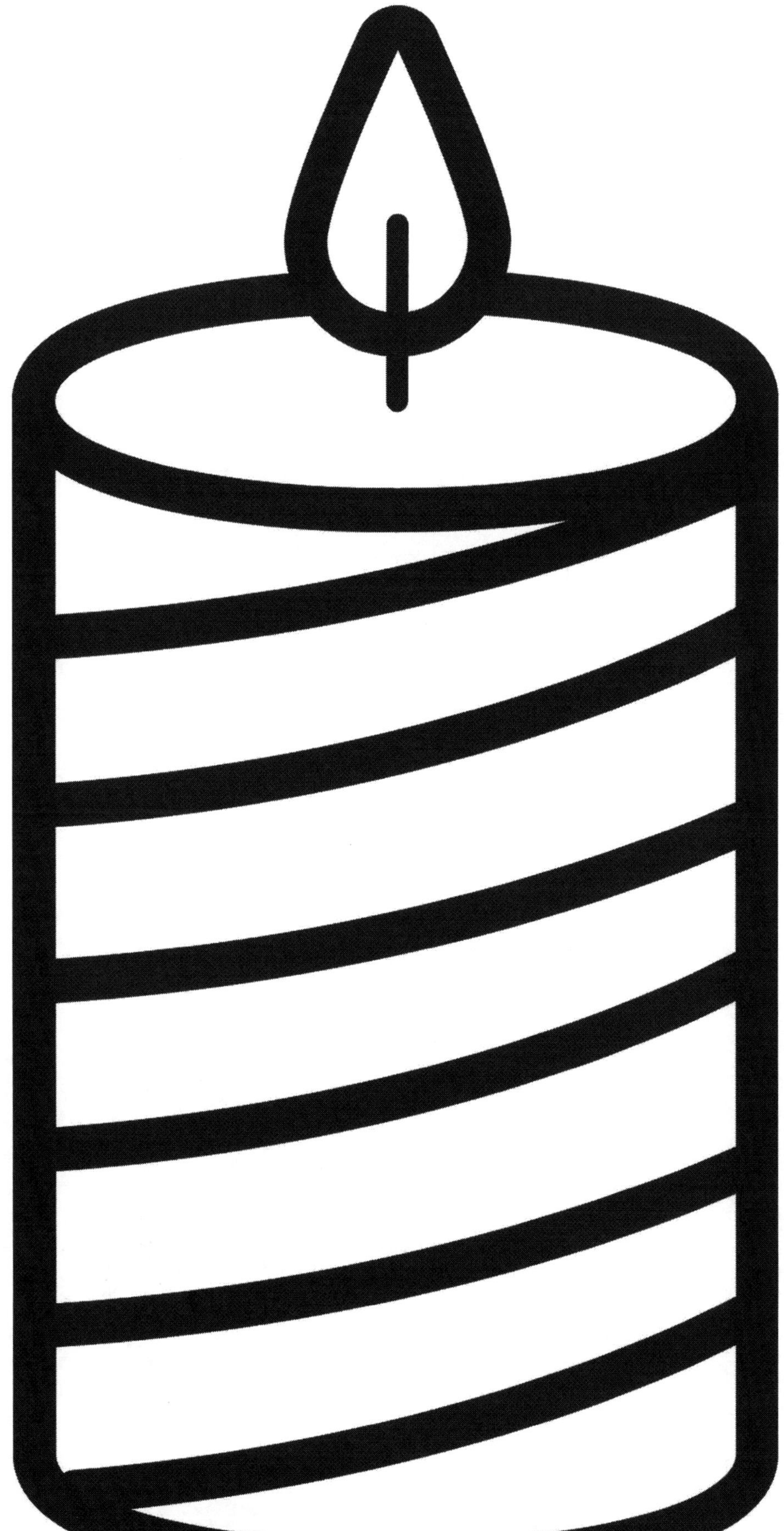

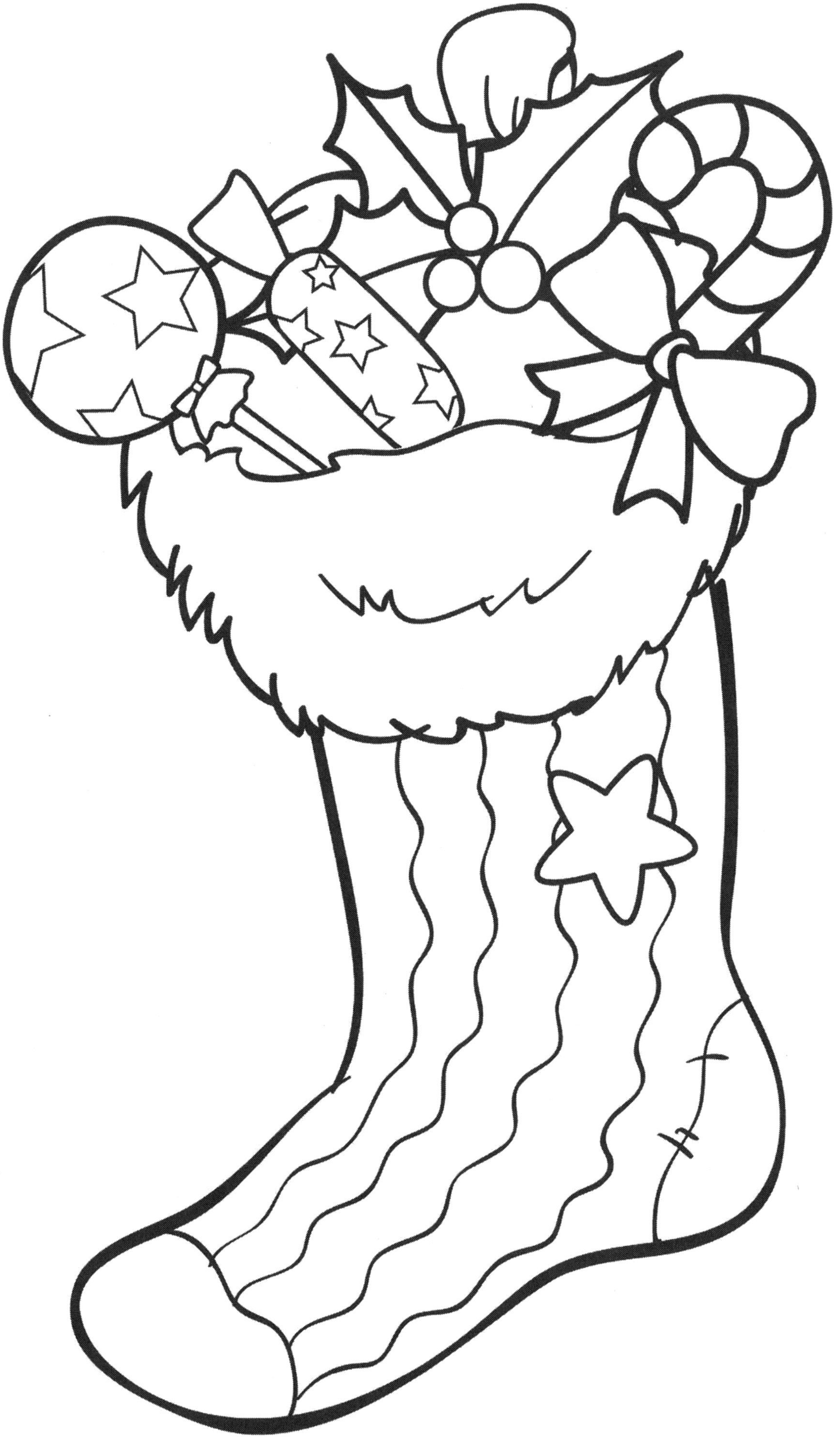

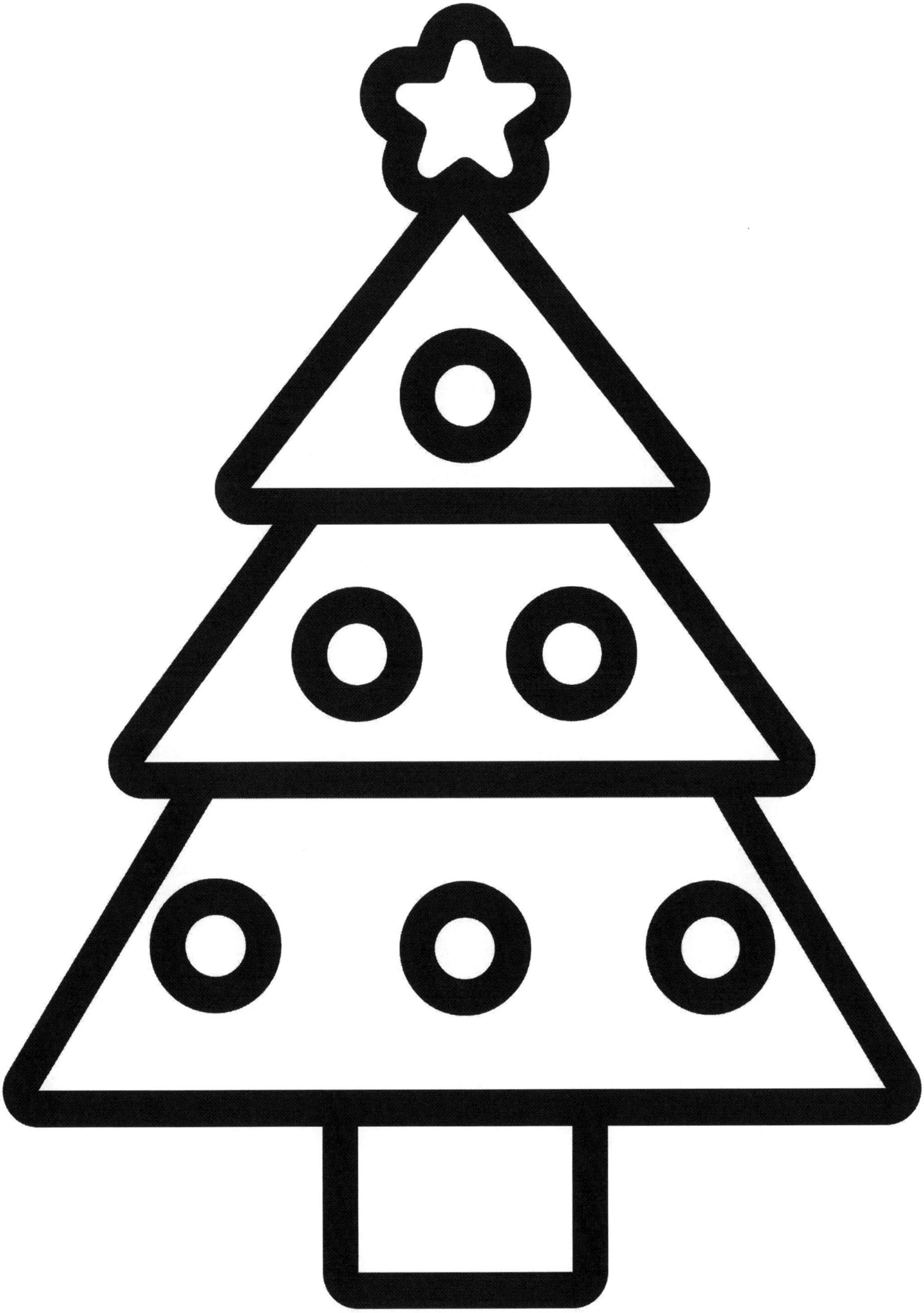

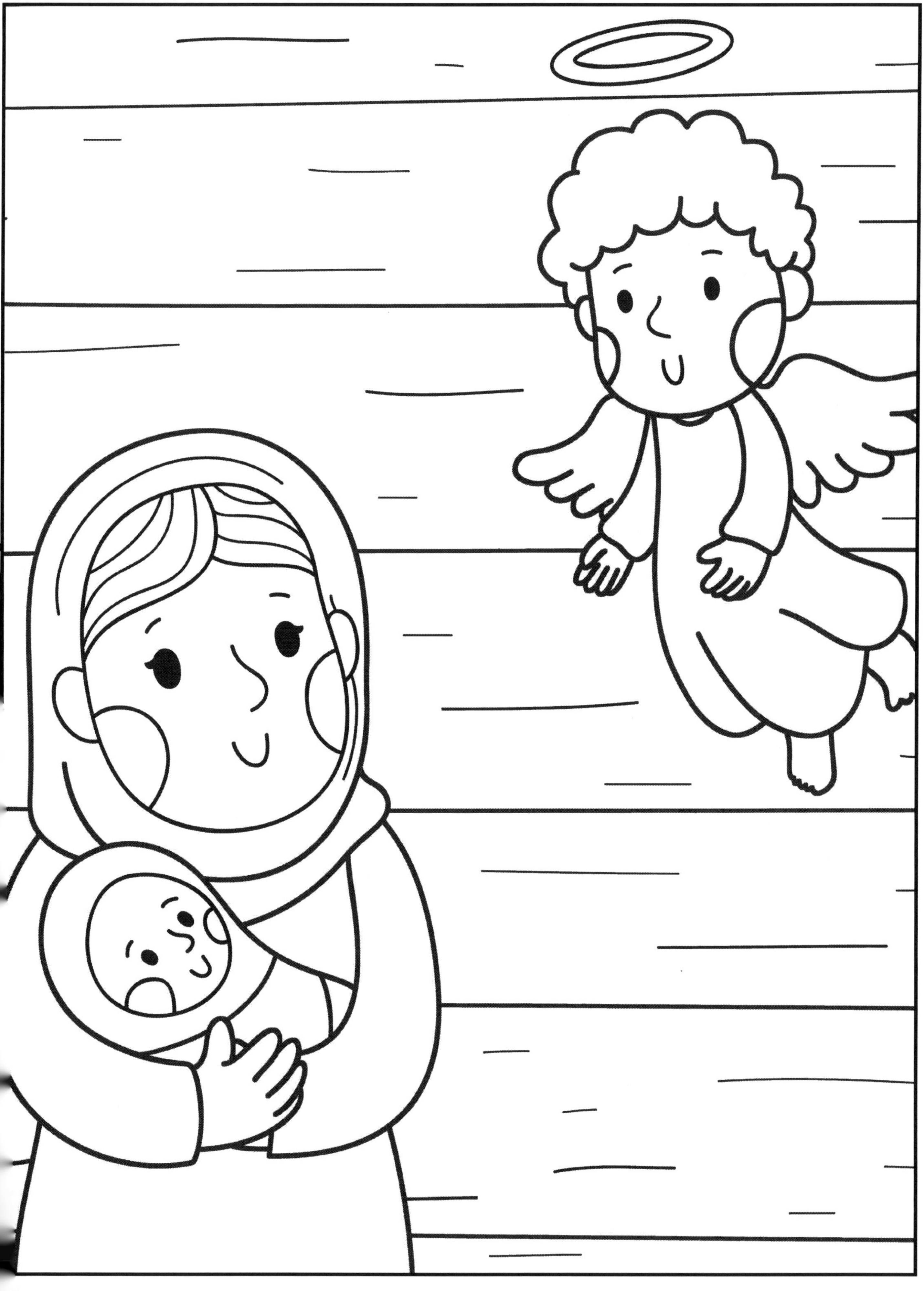

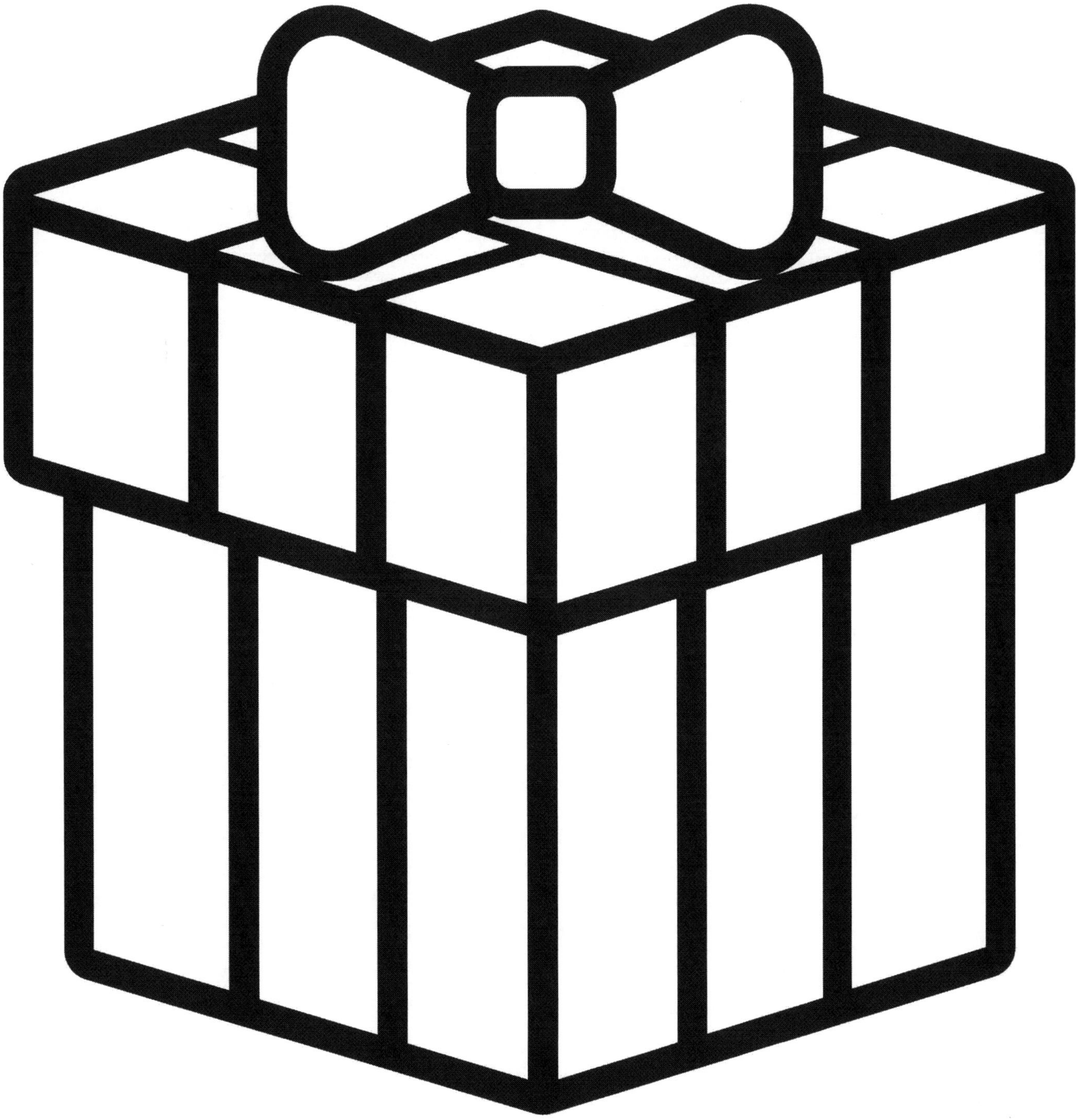

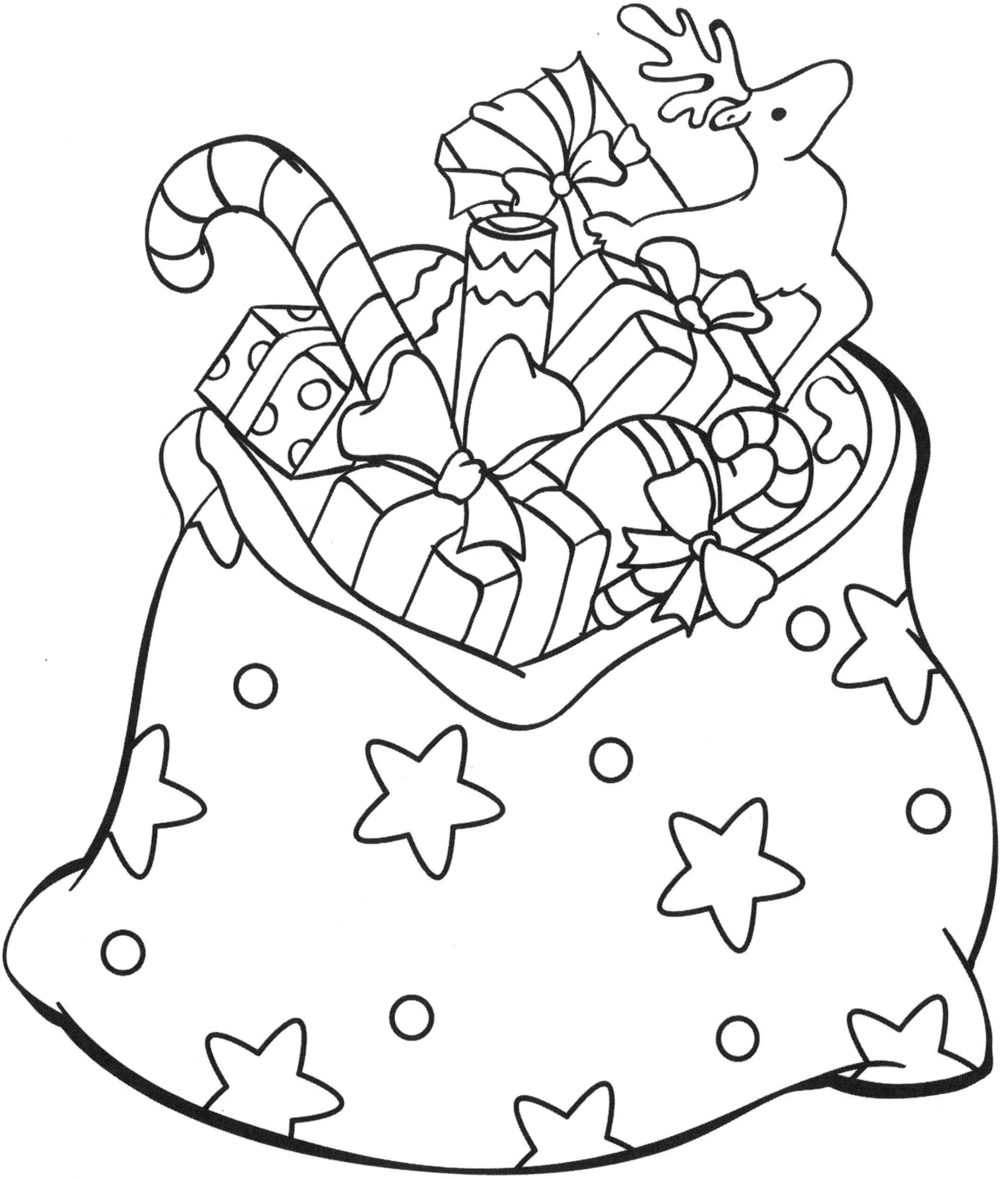

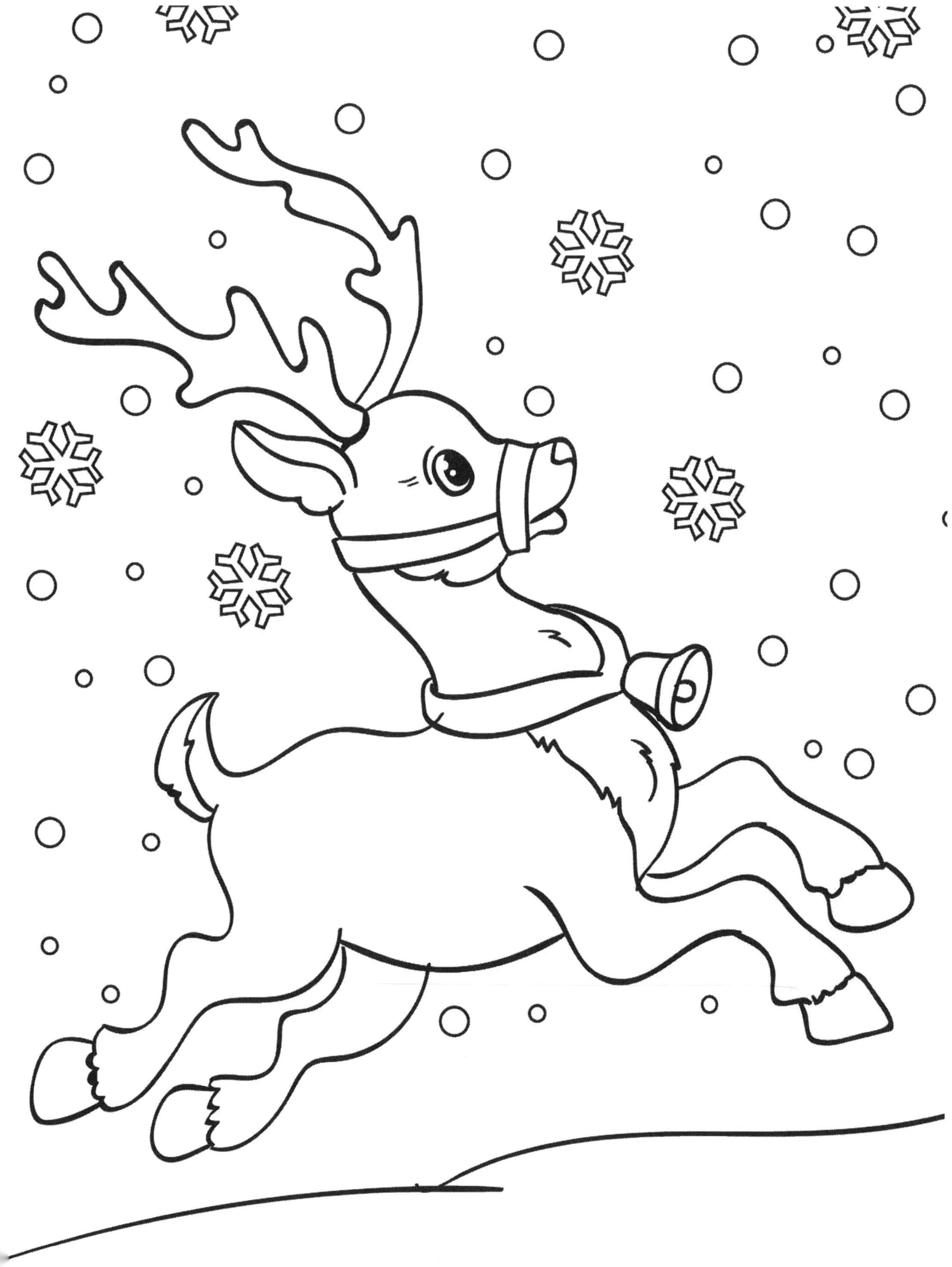

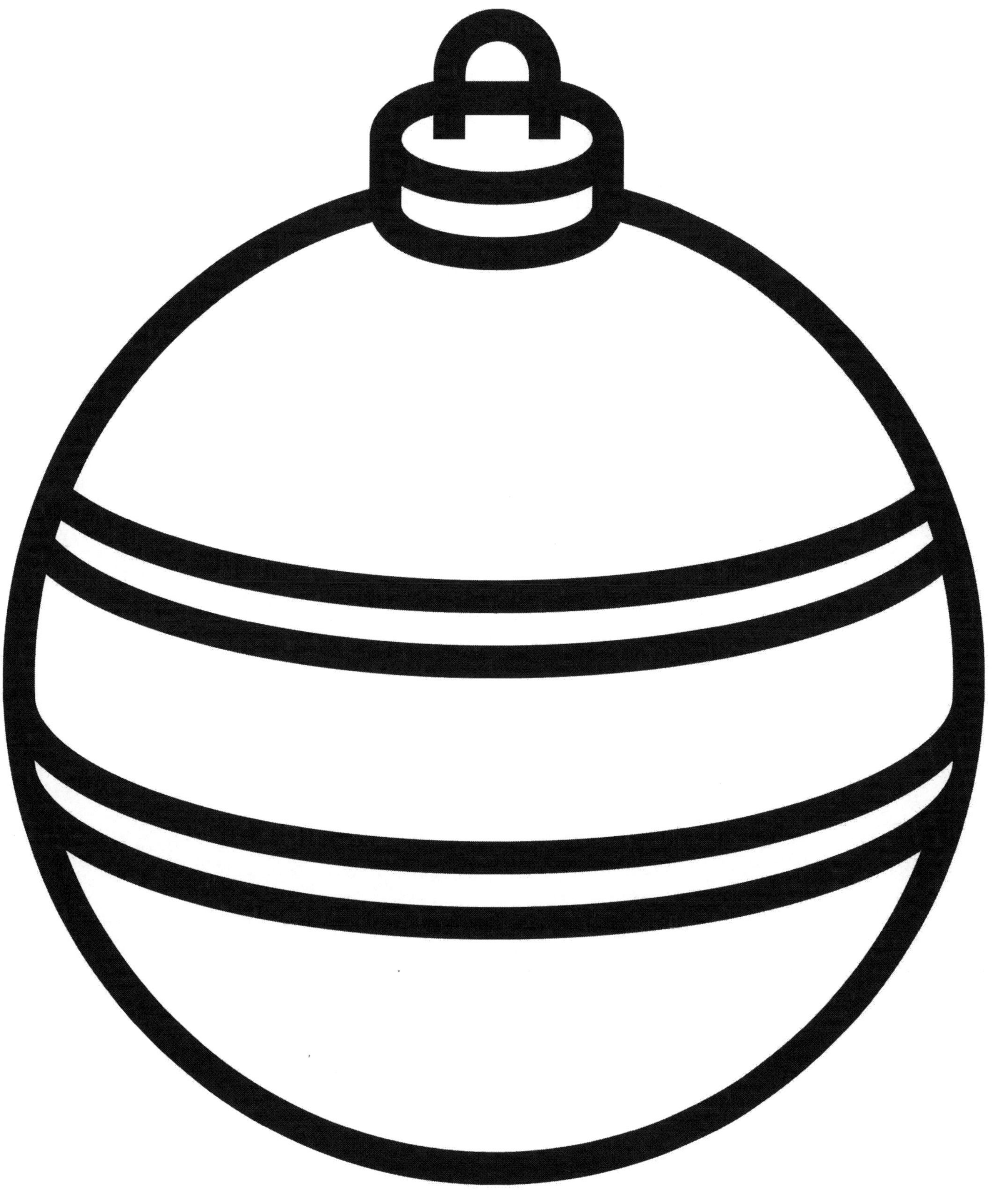

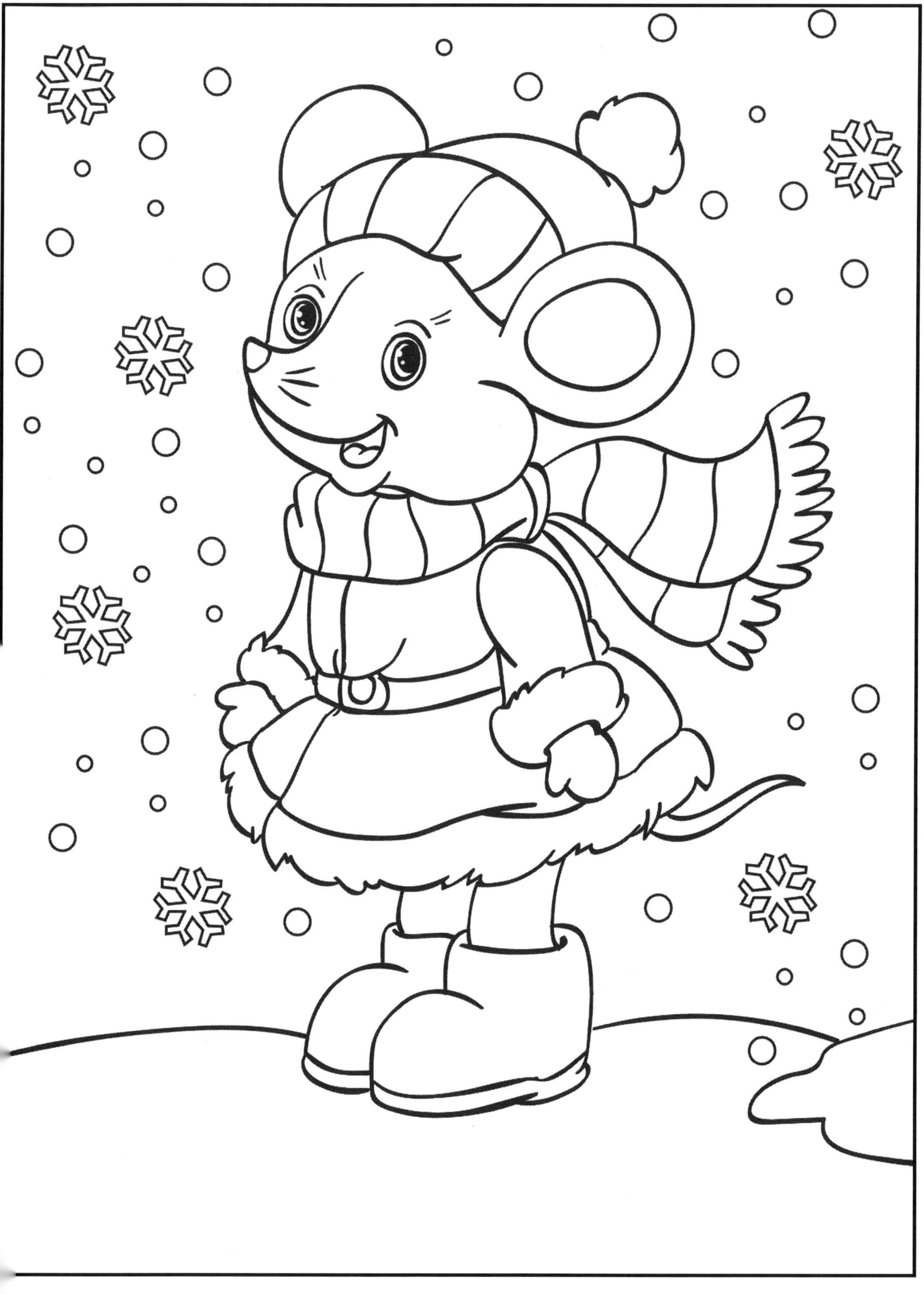

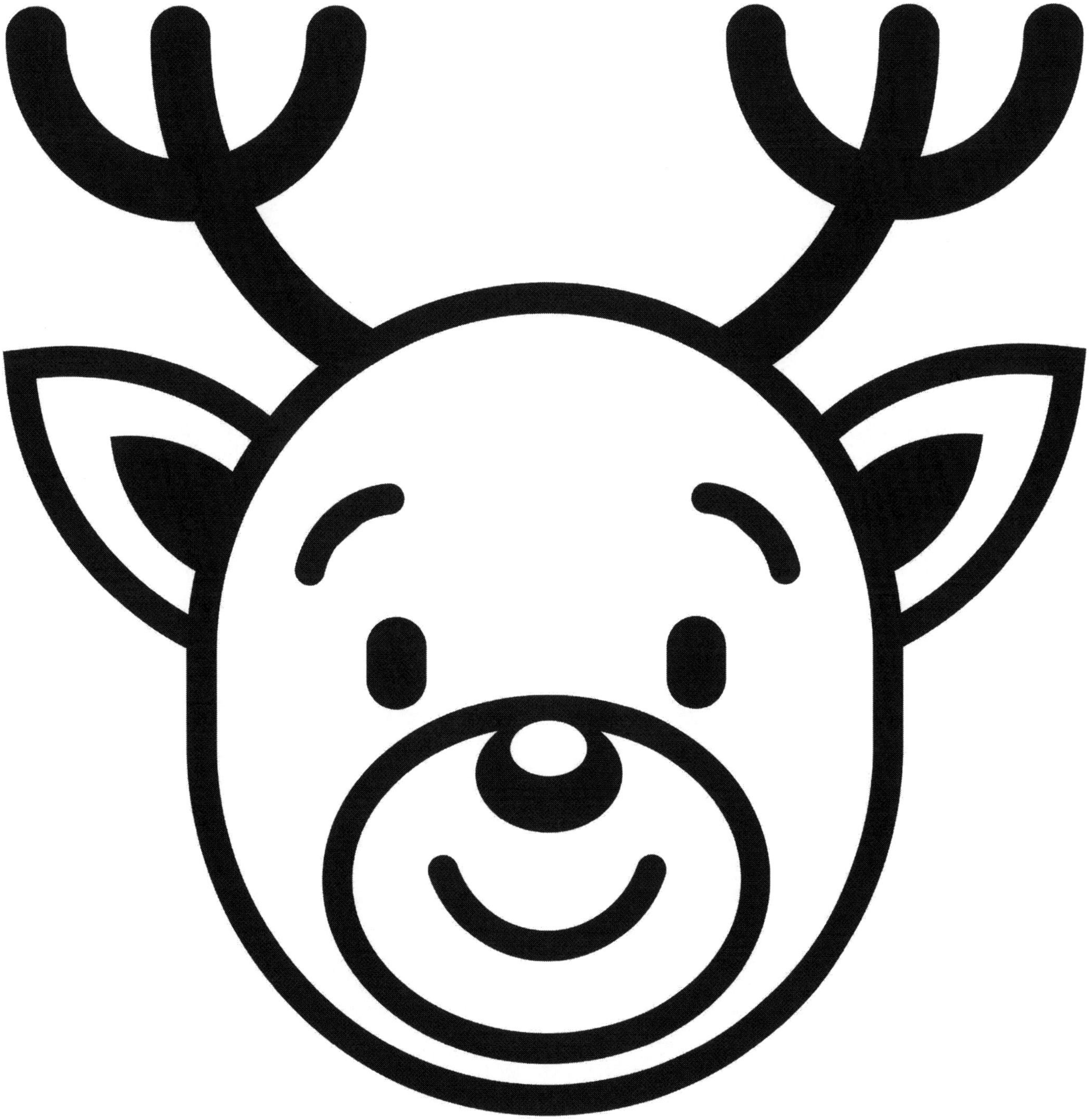

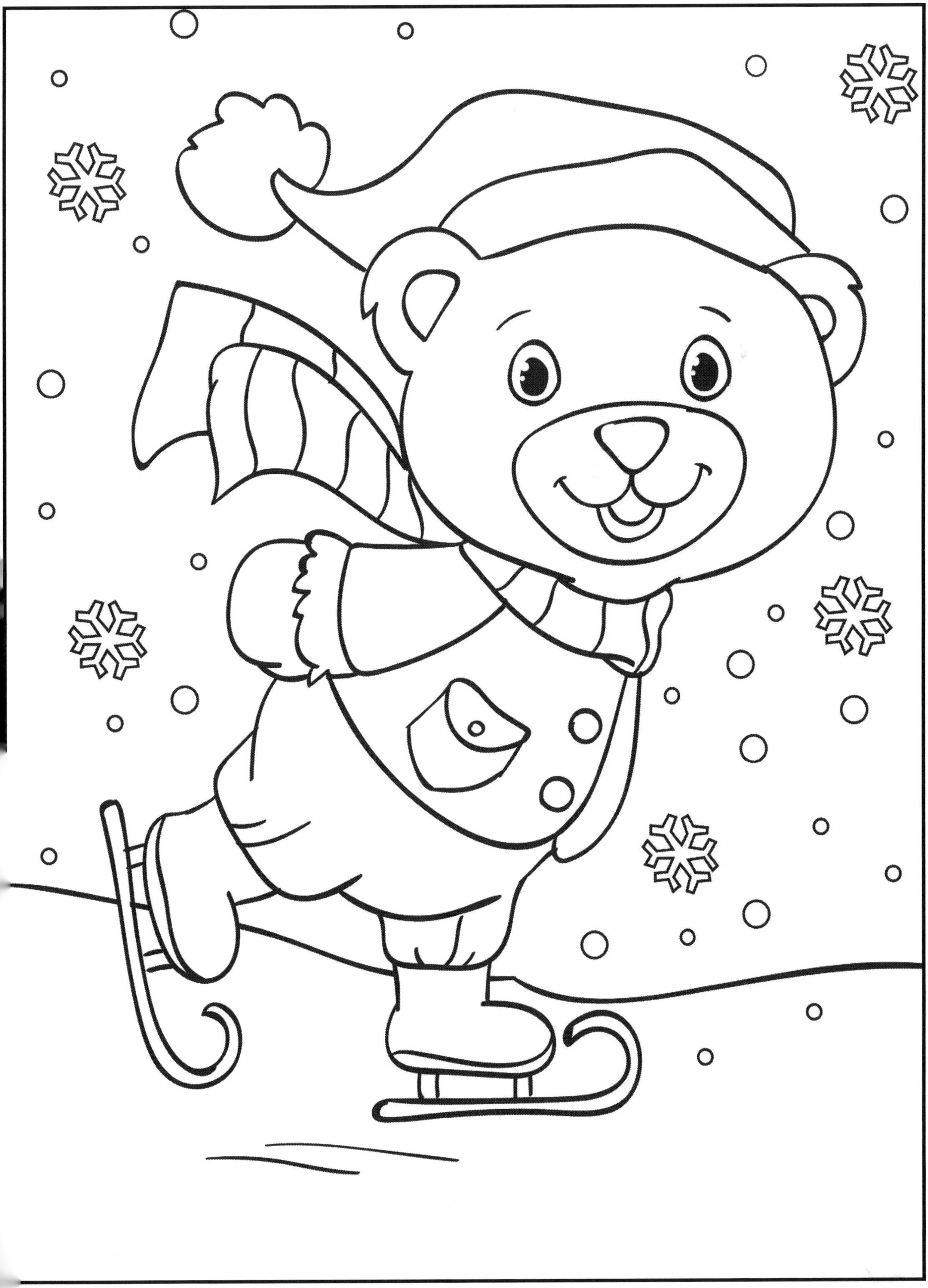

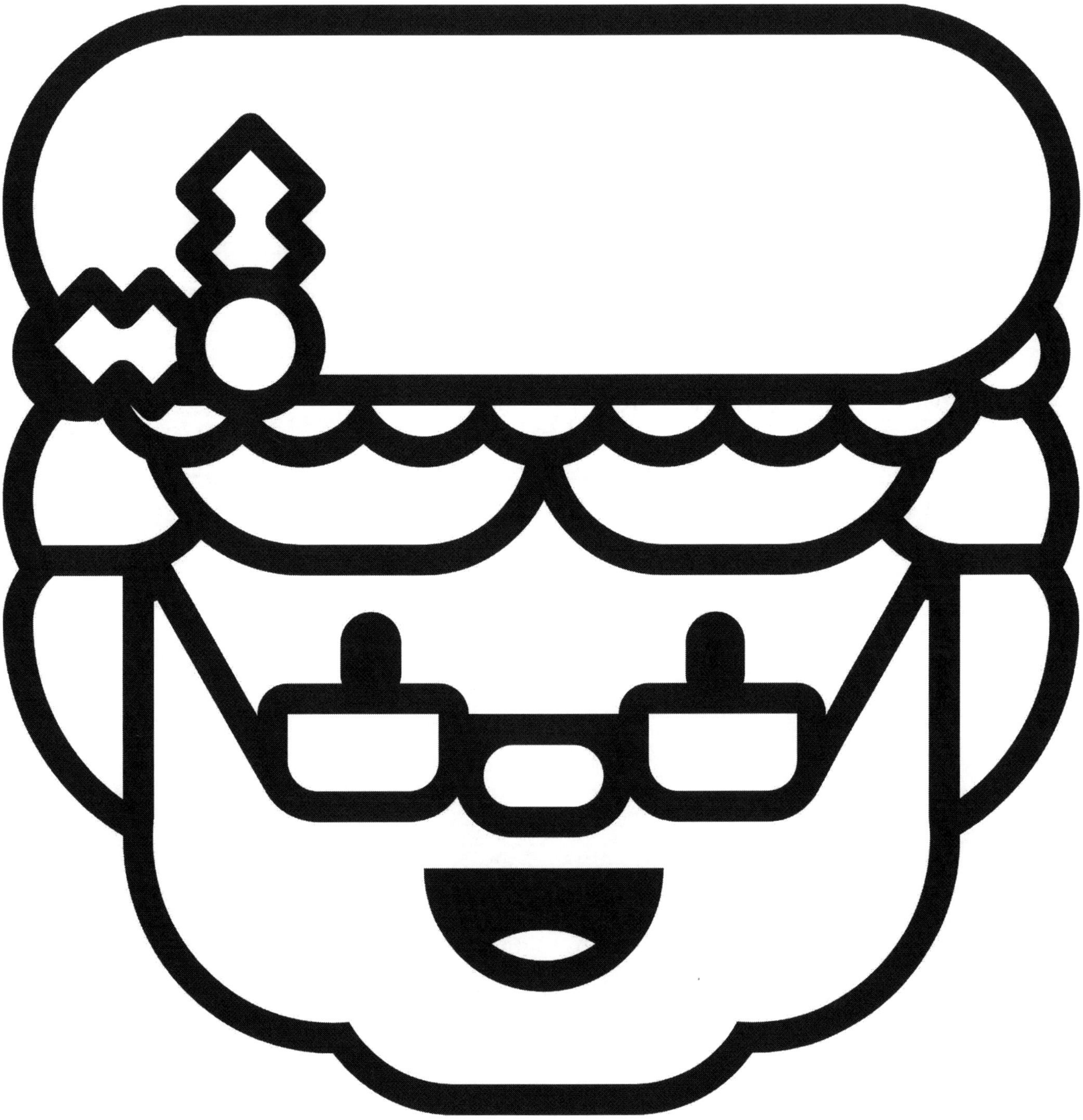

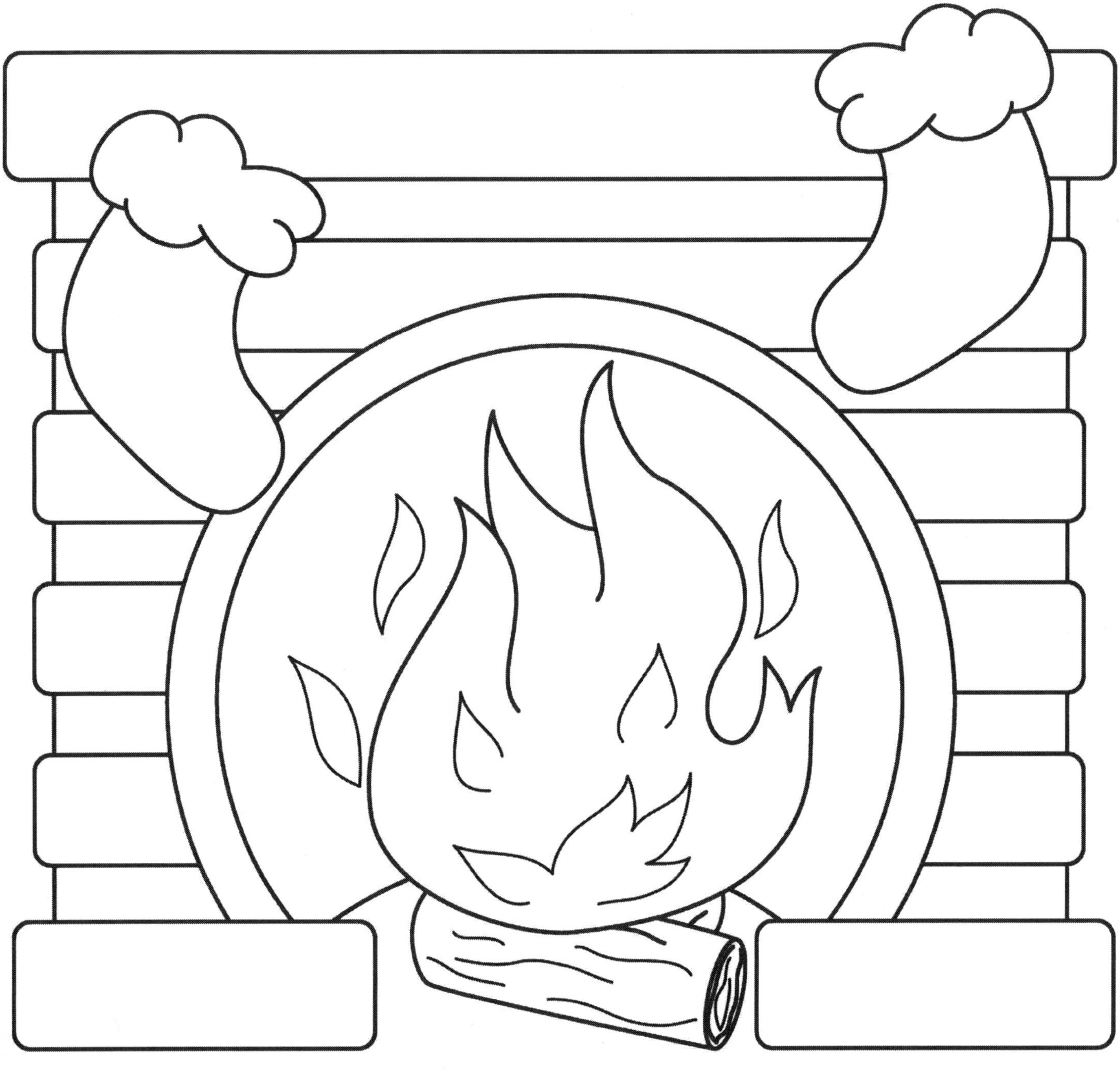

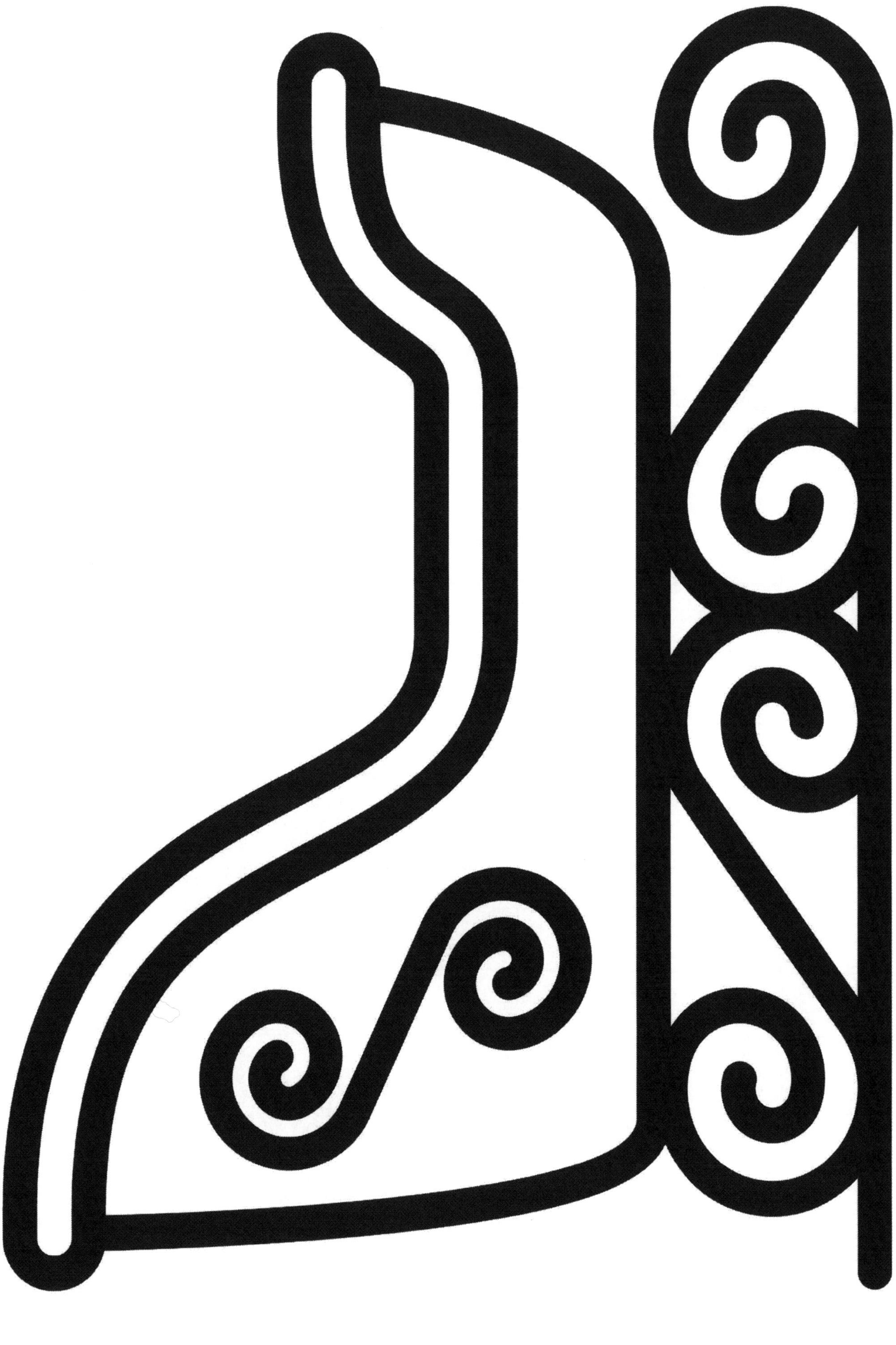

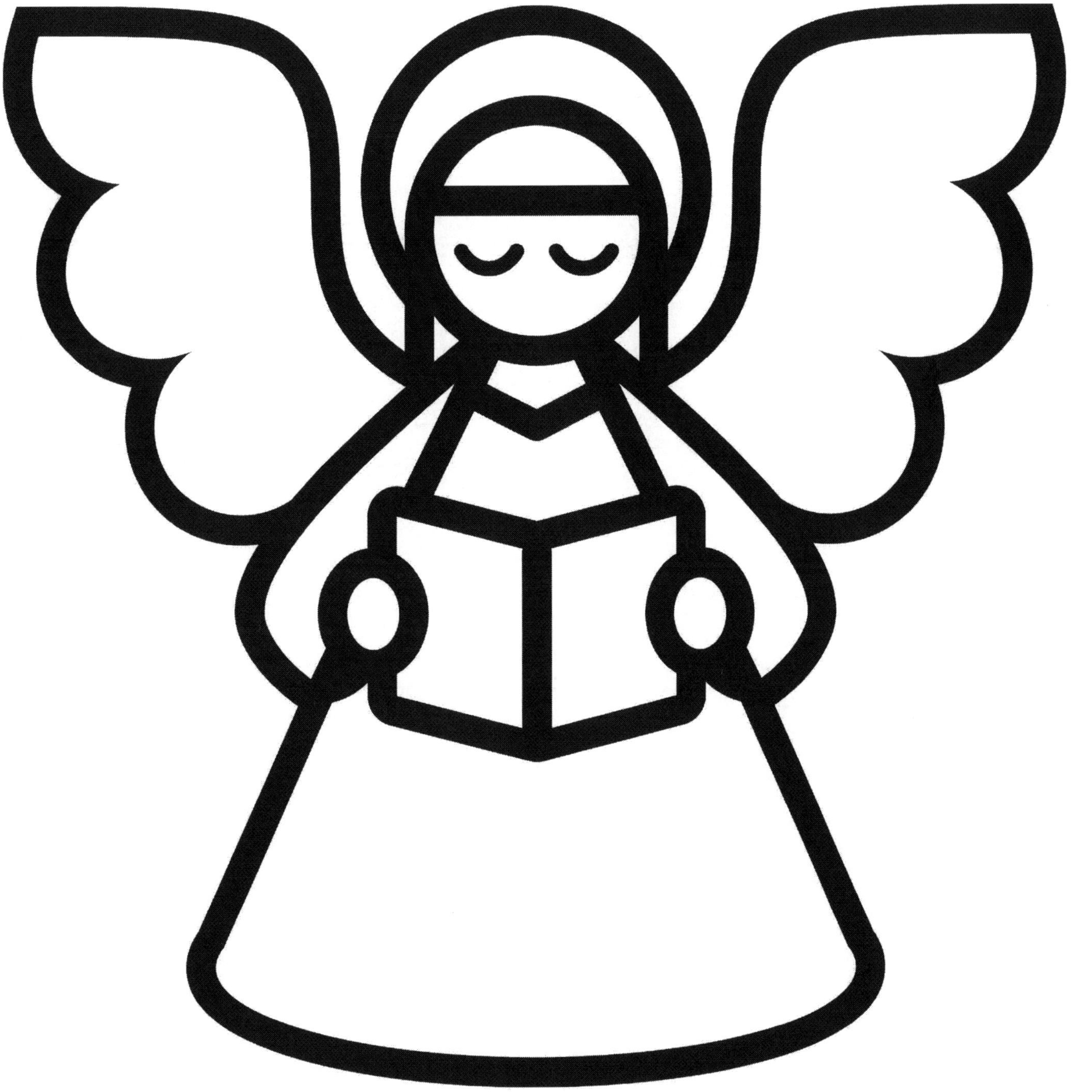

13258776R00075

Made in the USA
San Bernardino, CA
12 December 2018